literacy on display

Linda Duncan
Liz Webster

Acknowledgements

The authors and publishers would like to thank the children of The Vale First School and Aldingbourne Primary School for their co-operation in the making of this book. They would like to give special thanks to Sue Berry for her support and generosity in allowing them to use some of her work. They would also like to thank the Headteacher of The Vale School, Mr A Lovatt, and the Headteacher of Aldingbourne School, Mr P Neale. Finally, they would like to thank Ian Duncan for all his efforts and support in helping to produce this book and Steve Forest, the photographer, for his endless patience, good humour and for the excellent quality of photographs.

Daffodils (page 23)

First published in 2002 by BELAIR PUBLICATIONS LIMITED
Apex Business Centre, Boscombe Road, Dunstable, Beds, LU5 4RL

© 2002 Folens on behalf of the authors Linda Duncan and Liz Webster

Commissioning Editor: Karen McCaffery
Design: Jane Conway
Illustrators: Sara Silcock (Linda Rogers Associates) line drawings p13;
　　　　　　 Jane Conway p40.

Editor: Elizabeth Miles
Cover design: Ed Gallagher
Photography: Steve Forest
　　　　　　　 Kelvin Freeman

Belair books are protected by international copyright laws. All rights are reserved. The copyright of all materials in this book, except where otherwise stated, remains the property of the publisher and authors. No part of this publication may be reproduced, stored in a retrieval system, or transmitted, in any form or by any means, for whatever purpose, without the written permission of Belair Publications Limited.

Aztec Drinking Chocolate recipe from The Spice of Life by Kay Dunbar, Belair Publications Limited, 1992. The Kind Christmas Tree reproduced by permission from Anne English. Every effort has been made to contact copyright holders of material used in this book. If any have been overlooked, we will be pleased to make the necessary arrangements.

ISBN 0 94788 296 0

The cover photograph is taken from page 50.

Contents

Introduction	4
A is for Africa	6
The Bad-Tempered Ladybird	8
Bear in a Square	10
Big Bad Bill	12
Big Blue Whale	14
Breakfast	16
A Butterfly is Born	18
Daedalus and Icarus	20
Daffodils	22
The Drop Goes Plop	24
Elmer	26
The Enormous Crocodile	28
The Golden Tickets!	30
Handa's Surprise	32
Hurry, Santa!	34
In the Garden	36
The Jolly Postman	38
The Kind Christmas Tree	40
Leaping Frogs	42
The Little Red Hen	44
The Magic Bicycle	46
Mrs Armitage on Wheels	48
Mrs Jolly's Brolly	50
Oliver's Vegetables	52
Once Upon a Time	54
Penguins	56
Piggy Wiggy Fireman	58
The Rainbow Fish	60
Sam's Sandwich	62
The Star That Fell	64
The Tower to the Sun	66
The Very Hungry Caterpillar	68
Winter Morning	70
Book Lists	72

Introduction

Welcome to *Literacy on Display*. We hope you will find the ideas in this book stimulating and useful.

Display should be valued and seen not as a wall-covering exercise but as a valuable tool to enhance children's learning in literacy and other curriculum areas. What is the purpose of display?

Display quality work

Inspire children

Stimulate interest

Purposeful

Lively literacy

Attractive

Yield success

Why are Literacy Displays so Important?

It is essential that we maintain a high quality of literacy display in order to emphasise the importance of the teaching and learning of literacy. All schools should provide a rich and stimulating literacy environment and this can be achieved through excellent display that celebrates the children's success in literacy!

- Displays can be used by the children to enhance their literacy learning.
- They show that we value the children's work and in turn children will learn to respect and value each other's work.
- They allow us to share high-quality literacy work with others.
- They are a way of demonstrating the high quality of teaching and learning in literacy that is occurring throughout your school or classroom.
- They provide a stimulating and challenging environment and one in which children will thrive.

Literacy themes can be linked to other curriculum subjects and are often a stimulus for developing and extending knowledge in other areas. For example, *The Bad-Tempered Ladybird* can become a means of teaching the subject of time in Mathematics or *The Magic Bicycle* can be used for its strong geographical links.

Recording and Presenting Children's Literacy Work

Children's literacy work should be presented using varied and interesting formats.

- Present work on shaped paper relevant to the subject, for example a piece of descriptive writing about the Enormous Crocodile could be written on crocodile-shaped paper.
- Make a variety of book styles, such as zigzag, lift-the-flap, pop-up or shaped books for the children to write a piece of fiction or non-fiction work, such as a sandwich-shaped book (see page 63).
- Present work in the form of posters, leaflets, postcards, letters, diaries, lists, menus, instructions, games and recipes.

Literacy Wall displays

To ensure interesting and effective literacy displays:

- Have a central focus for displays.
- Use attractive backing papers in interesting ways, such as a chequer-board pattern.
- Choose colours appropriate to the subject. Work with a limited range of colours.
- Use a variety of different borders to hide untidy edges. Try to relate borders to the display topic.
- Show a variety of children's work on each display.
- Ensure the work is of a high quality so that the children want to read it.
- Use informative and relevant labelling, and laminate labels so that they can be used again.
- Use a variety of lettering styles and computer fonts large enough for the children to read. Enlarge the labels to an appropriate size using a photocopier.
- Involve children in writing the labels.
- Use appropriate literacy words, such as fiction, non-fiction, contents, glossary, author, illustrator and blurb, so that the children can use these words to extend their knowledge.
- Give displays a 3D effect; bow out the pictures and labels.
- Use staples or reusable adhesive rather than drawing pins.

Literacy Table-top Displays

Use table-top displays to provide a link to wall displays and allow the children to interact practically with them. Table-top displays could include:

- the book studied to encourage children to enjoy the text again
- a tape recorder to provide the children with the opportunity to respond to the text or listen to the story
- plants, artefacts, children's work, questions and activities as appropriate.

First impressions are vital and everlasting. It is important that display captures the children's imagination and inspires them to want to achieve the best they can. Good displays do take time but the end result is worthwhile and very rewarding.

A is for Africa

Literacy

- **Non-fiction:** *A is for Africa* by Ifeoma Onyefulu.
- Display pictures and clues about Africa around the classroom. Take the children on an imaginary journey to Africa pointing out the landmarks and animals displayed. Ask the children to write creatively about their African experience.
- Write a postcard to a friend from Africa explaining what you have seen and experienced.
- Compose African landmark anagrams.
- Design a poster advertising a holiday in Africa.
- Write a list of things you would take on holiday to Africa.
- Use the text to write a comparative poem about life in your own country compared with life in Africa, for example,

    *An African house is made of mud
    My house is made of bricks.
    The children travel to school by canoe
    I walk to school or travel by car.*

- Make an alphabet book in the same style as *A is for Africa* based on countries of the world, 'A is for Australia, B is for Britain, C is for Canada' or about your own school, town or city.
- List the African countries in alphabetical order.

Poems and Rhymes

- 'Postcard' by Tony Langham, *An Orange Poetry Paintbox* selected by John Foster.
- 'When You go to Dance' by Okot p'Bitek (Uganda), *Talking Drums* selected by Veronique Tadjo.
- 'Civil Lies' by Benjamin Zephaniah, *The Puffin Book of Utterly Brilliant Poetry* selected by Brian Patten.

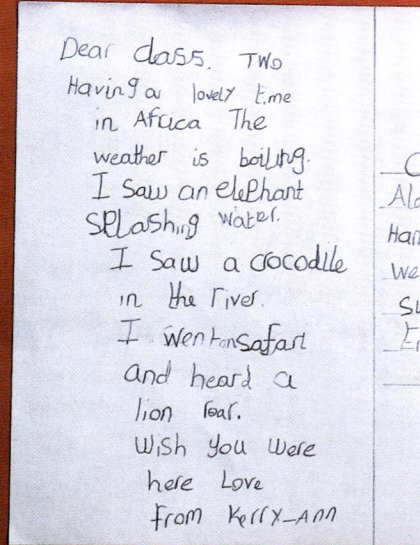
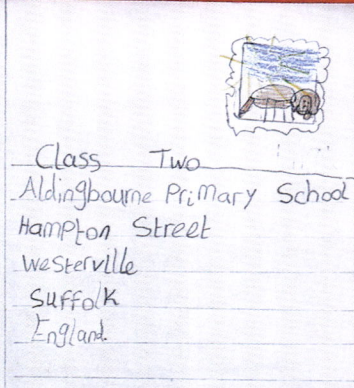

Art and Design Technology

- Design pictures for the front of a postcard from Africa.
- Tie-dye calico and use felt and threads to sew a picture that depicts African culture.
- Colour-mix warm African colours (reds, yellows and oranges).

- Use Modrock to make a map of Africa. Paint on the main oceans, rivers and mountain ranges.
- Make African jewellery, decorated head bands, and beads made from clay or salt dough.
- Model African pots from clay.

Information Technology

- Use the internet to research information about Africa.
- Encourage the children, working in groups, to use a range of equipment (computer, overhead projector, video, tape recorder or camera) to make a presentation about Africa or an African country.

Geography

- Locate Africa on a world map. Find out the names of countries that make up Africa.
- Use a map of Africa and ask the children to locate different landmarks using simple co-ordinates, for example, River Niger, Mount Kilimanjaro, Sahara Desert and Victoria Falls.

Dance, Drama and Role Play

- Listen to 'Sunchyme' (Single) by Dario G, (WEA, 1997). Use empty aluminium cans to create an African-style dance. Tap the cans to the rhythm of the music, following a sequence: tap cans above the head, in front of the body, behind the body, between the legs.
- Create a travel agency corner. Use holiday brochures and computers to book a holiday to Africa.

The Bad-Tempered Ladybird

Literacy

- **Fiction:** *The Bad-Tempered Ladybird* by Eric Carle.
- Ask the children to write sentences about the animals the bad-tempered ladybird met at different times of the day (for example, 'At 8 o'clock she met a small stripy wasp …').
- Write a list of reasons to suggest why the ladybird might have come to the leaf in a bad temper.
- Write a letter to the bad-tempered ladybird expressing the children's concerns about her behaviour and suggesting how she might mend her ways.
- Find other compound words and write them on ladybird-shaped paper.
- Ask the children what they think of the bad-tempered ladybird's behaviour and manners. Use the letters from the word 'ladybird' to write a message explaining how we should treat each other, for example, '**L**ove all creatures. **A**lways protect one another. **D**on't be cruel. **Y**ou must be kind...' and so on.
- How might the creatures in the story help the bad-tempered ladybird get in a better mood? What could each animal do to try to help, for example, have a party, go to sleep, sing a song.

Poems and Rhymes

- 'Ladybug' by Joan Walsh Anglund, *Mini Beasties* selected by Michael Rosen.
- 'Hurt No Living Thing' by Christina Rosetti, *Scholastic Collections – Poetry* selected by Wes Magee.

Art and Design Technology

- Use chalk pastels to draw ladybirds.
- Colour mix shades of red paint onto giant ladybird-shaped paper.
- Paint pictures of the other creatures featured in the story.
- Model ladybirds using clay.

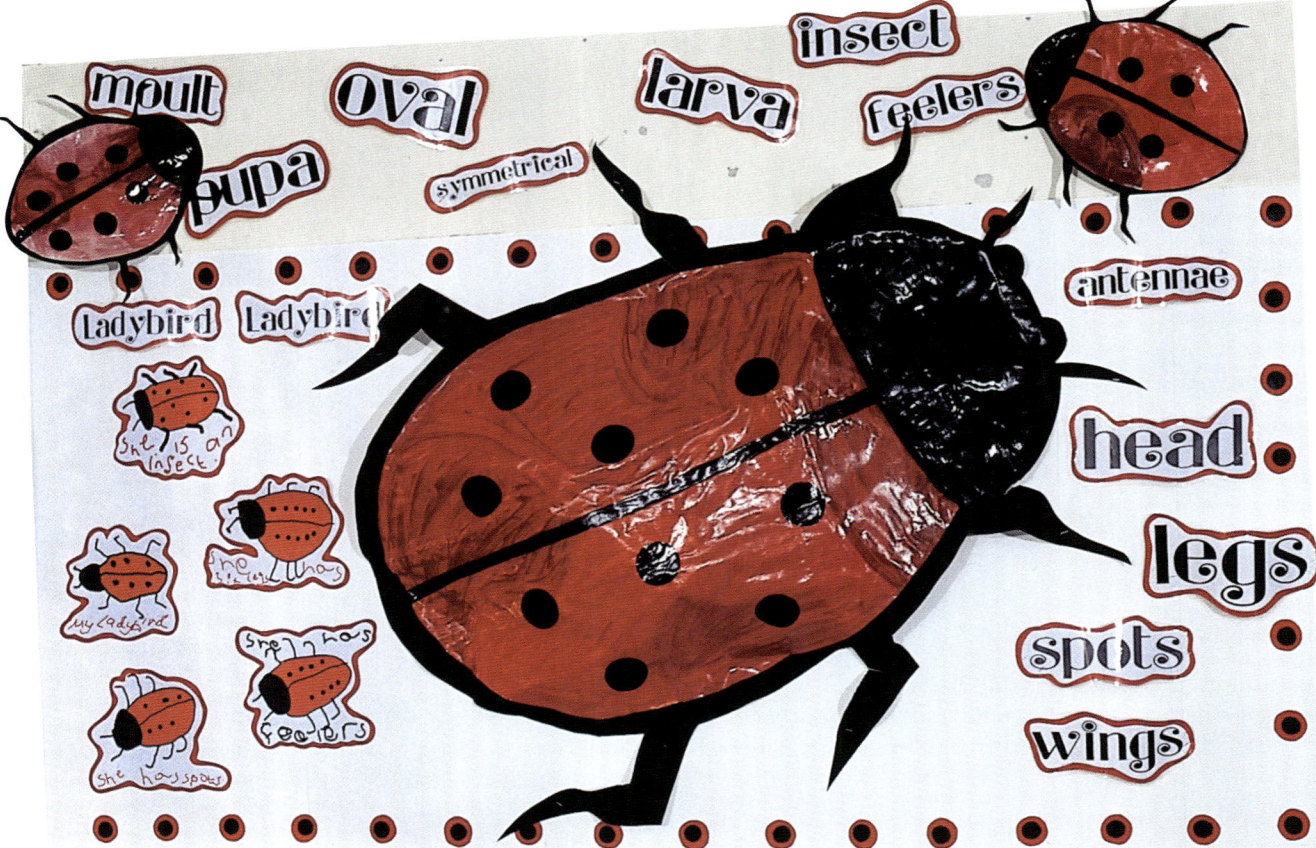

Mathematics

- Sequence the pictures from the story according to the time of day.
- Ask the children to make their own clocks. Encourage them to move the hands on the clocks showing the different times featured in the story.
- Set time problems, for example, 'If the ladybird met the wasp at 8 o'clock, who did she meet 1 hour later? 1 hour earlier?'
- Make and play a ladybird domino game, matching the number of spots on their backs.
- Count in 6s: 1 ladybird has 6 legs, 2 ladybirds have 12 legs ... . How many legs do 20 ladybirds have?

Science

- Research the life cycle of a ladybird and compare with the life cycle of another insect featured in the story.
- Observe ladybirds in their natural environment. Look carefully at their body structure and how they move.

Information Technology

- Use a programmable toy such as Roamer or Pixie to retell the story of *The Bad-Tempered Ladybird*. Transform the Roamer into a ladybird by adding black spots and program the Roamer or Pixie to visit the different characters.

Bear in a Square

Literacy

- **Fiction:** *Bear in a Square* by Stella Blackstone.
- Find words that rhyme with 'square' and write them on square paper. Use the words to find alternative titles for the book, for example, Pear in a Square, Chair in a Square.
- Write a story in the same style as *Bear in a Square* perhaps using 3D shapes, for example, Deer in a Sphere or Fox in a Box.
- Write a list of objects that are a particular shape, for example, a circle – clock, plate, saucer.
- Write sentences about shapes, focusing on the properties of shapes and on sentence structure. Compile these into a Fact Finder Shape booklet.
- Make a rhyming zigzag book. Include the rhyming word families, such as 'The CAT in the HAT SAT on a MAT and spoke to the BAT who was rather FAT and THAT was THAT!'
- Create a rhyming shape poem using different shapes and simple rhyming words.
- Work in small groups and write a story based on your shape puppets (see Art and Design Technology).

Art and Design Technology

- Make shape pictures using paper collage.
- Look at the work of the artist Kandinsky and create pictures in a similar style using the shapes featured in the story.
- Print shape patterns using a variety of different shapes.
- Make shape mobiles using the shapes featured in the story *Bear in a Square*.
- Design and make 2D-shape puppets using the shapes featured in the story.
- Design and make a model using 3D construction shapes. Label all the shapes used.

Mathematics

- Identify and investigate the properties of 2D and 3D shapes.
- Devise sequencing patterns using 2D and 3D shapes.
- Find out which of the shapes featured in the story will tessellate.
- Count the number of shapes featured on each page of the story. Plot the results as a graph.

Science

- Investigate how to change the shape of different objects, such as empty tin cans, elastic bands, paper, and cardboard boxes.
- Investigate how the shapes of materials and food change if they are heated or cooled, such as chocolate, jelly and ice cubes.

Information Technology

- Learn to draw 2D shapes using a computer drawing package. Draw shape pictures.

Geography

- Organise a 'Shape Hunt' around school to identify shapes in the environment.

Big Bad Bill

Literacy

- **Fiction:** *Big Bad Bill* by Martin Waddell.
- Ask the children to look for words ending in 'ck'. Write them on Bill's sack.
- Make a list of words that rhyme with 'Bill'. Invent silly sentences about Bill using these words.
- Discuss the meaning of the word 'swag' – write a list of Bill's swag that he collected from the mill.
- The children can use their own names to create an alliterative name like 'Big Bad Bill'.
- Make a character study of Big Bad Bill. Brainstorm words to describe Bill's character and features. Write the words around a picture of Bill.
- Create a 'Wanted' poster warning people about Big Bad Bill.
- Ask the children to retell the story of *Big Bad Bill* in their own words. Present their writing on windmill-shaped paper.

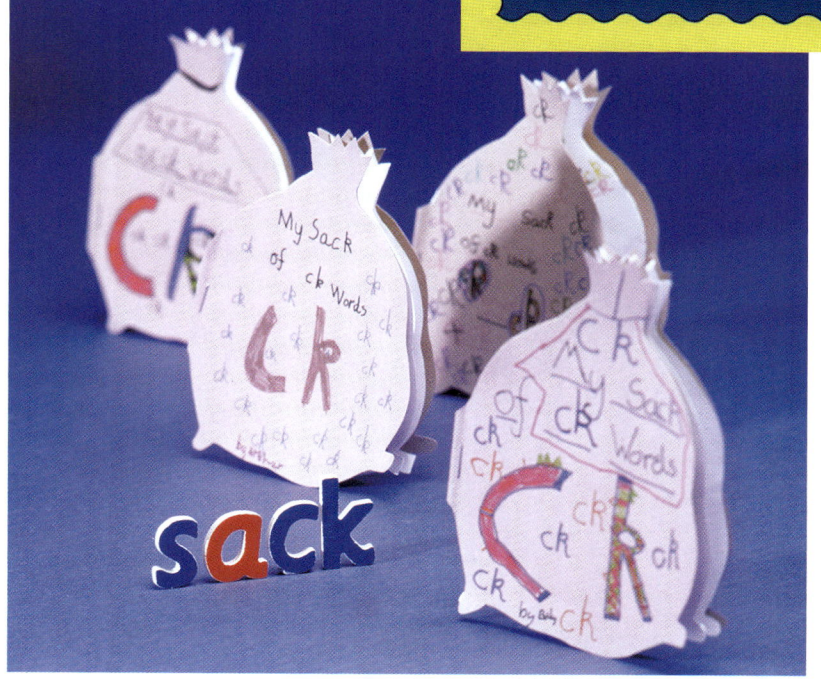

- Discuss 'Nobody' with the children. Who do they think he is? Did he used to work there? Ask the children to compose their own ideas about who 'Nobody' is.
- Write letters to Big Bad Bill explaining the wrongs of stealing and suggesting how he might reform.
- Design a leaflet about windmills and include a written description of how a windmill works.

Art and Design Technology

- Draw or paint pictures of Big Bad Bill.
- Print with cogs of different sizes on paper or fabric to create a large machine or cut cogs out of different papers or fabrics to create a collage.
- Use a computer drawing package to create a 'Wanted' poster for Big Bad Bill. Explore the use of different fonts and colours.
- Design and make a windmill using construction kits or recycled material.
- Make windmills from bright coloured paper or card. Test outside on a windy day.

1. On a large square of coloured paper cut from each corner almost to the centre.

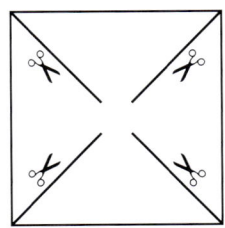

2. Fold over each wing and join at the centre.

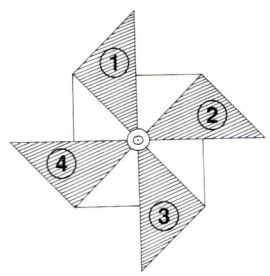

Mathematics

- Use paper windmills to demonstrate rotational symmetry. Label the sails with the numbers 1 to 4 and rotate each sail through 90°.
- Make sacks of different weights and sizes. Encourage the children to arrange them according to weight and size. Estimate the weights of each sack.

Personal, Social and Health Education

- Teacher adopts the role of Big Bad Bill and encourages the children to ask Bill questions about his behaviour. Focus on the theme of stealing and 'right and wrong'.
- Discuss with the children how they could help Bill to become a good citizen. Compile a list of rules, for example, a good citizen should help his friends, co-operate with others ... and so on.

Big Blue Whale

Literacy

- **Non-fiction:** *Big Blue Whale* by Nicola Davies.
- Write 'wh' words on small whale-shaped paper.
- Ask the children to work in groups and brainstorm anything they know about whales. Record on large whale-shaped paper.
- After reading the text, write additional knowledge on the back of the whale-shaped paper.
- Use the information to make a Whale Facts leaflet.
- Use a dictionary or glossary to find out the meaning of words such as krill, blubber, mammal, baleen plates and fin.
- Make up similes to describe features of the whale, for example 'skin as soft and bouncy as jelly'.
- Write a letter to Greenpeace or the International Whaling Commission asking for more information about their work.
- Match homonyms (for example, Wales, whales; see, sea). Ask the children to give a definition for each word.

Poems and Rhymes

- 'The Song of the Whale' by Kit Wright, *Scholastic Collections – Poetry* selected by Wes Magee.
- 'If You Ever' – Anon, *Poems for the Very Young* selected by Michael Rosen.
- 'Blue Whale' by Giles Andreae and David Wojtowycz, *Commotion in the Ocean*.

Art and Design Technology

- Draw chalk pastel whale pictures.
- Model whales from clay.
- Dribble PVA glue onto calico to form a whale shape. When it is dry use fabric paints to colour the whale and the sea.
- Paint pictures of the sea, using thick paint and palette knives to create wave effects.

Information Technology

- Use the internet to research information about whales.
- Visit the Greenpeace website at www.Greenpeace.org.
- Use a computer draw package to draw and label a big blue whale.

Geography

- Find out where whales live and breed.
- Use a world map to plot the migration route of the blue whale.

Personal, Social and Health Education

- Read the story *Jonah and the Whale* by Geoffrey Patterson.
- Use the letters in the word 'whale' to encourage the children to work hard and be kind to others:

  Work hard
  Help each other
  Ask a friend for help
  Learn to be kind to each other
  Everybody should work together.

- Make laminated whale badges to give to the children if they display any of the above attributes. This could be called the 'Whale Award'.
- Discuss the issues of whaling. Talk about why whales are hunted and what their use is to people. Is whaling right? Debate the issue.

Breakfast

Literacy

- **Non-fiction:** *Breakfast – Discovery World* by David Flint.
- Look at the contents and index pages of *Breakfast* and discuss their use.
- Write a breakfast booklet to find out where a particular breakfast food or drink comes from. Use the same format as the text.
- Use a dictionary to define the word 'breakfast' and explore the meaning of 'break fast'.
- Make a list of foods eaten at breakfast time and put them in alphabetical order.
- Create a wordsearch of 'breakfast' words, such as cereal, milk, orange juice and eggs.
- Write a breakfast menu for your favourite breakfast.
- Use the letters in the word 'breakfast' to make as many new words as possible.
- Taste different cereals and think of words to describe the texture, smell and appearance, for example, crunchy, sweet, lumpy and soggy.

- **Fiction:** *The Magic Porridge Pot* by Joan Stimson.
- Retell the story *The Magic Porridge Pot* in your own words.
- As a starting point for creative writing ask the children to imagine what they would do if they came home from school to find their house or street covered in porridge. How would they get rid of it? Who would they ask to help them?
- Taste porridge and think of adjectives such as delicious, lovely, tasty and so on.

Poems and Rhymes

- 'The King's Breakfast' by AA Milne, *A Packet of Poems* selected by Jill Bennett.
- 'Breakfast' by Eleanor Farjeon, *A Packet of Poems* selected by Jill Bennett.
- 'Breakfast Time' by Michael Rosen, *Hard-boiled Legs – The Breakfast Book* by Michael Rosen.

Art and Design Technology

- Look closely at a variety of cereal packets. Design your own using pastels, pencil crayons and felt-tipped pens.
- Design and make a clay cereal bowl or an egg cup. Paint and glaze the finished design.
- Design and make a 'new' brand of cereal using a variety of grains, dried fruits and chopped fresh fruit. Taste and describe it.
- Have breakfast at school and make porridge for the event.

Mathematics

- Create a graph showing the children's favourite cereals. Ask questions based on the graph, for example, 'How many children like cornflakes more than muesli?'
- Weigh and balance different amounts of cereal using standard and non-standard measures.
- Open out a cereal box and look at the shape. Make a net of a cuboid to make your own cereal box.
- Collect empty cartons of milk and fruit juices. Compare and order their capacities.

Science

- Introduce the topic of healthy eating and discuss the importance of breakfast in providing enough energy for the day.
- Make a list of 'breakfast foods' and sort them into dairy products, carbohydrates and fats.

Information Technology

- Use the internet to research information about cereal, milk and orange juice.
- Use a word processing package to write sentences about breakfast. Encourage the children to use different fonts, colours and sizes.

A Butterfly is Born

Literacy

- **Non-fiction:** *A Butterfly is Born* by Melvin Berger.
- Make a list of all the facts the children have learnt from reading the text.
- Write factual sentences about caterpillars and butterflies.
- Write butterfly acrostics, for example:

  Beautiful butterfly
  Up and down they flutter
  Turning
  Twisting
  Everywhere
  Radiant colours
  Flying high in the sky
  Laying eggs on tiny leaves
  Yummy nectar good to taste.

- Create a 'compound word hunt' around the school. Ask the children to find the two words that make one compound word when they are put together. Examples are: butter and fly, lady and bird, basket and ball.
- Write anagrams using words relevant to caterpillars and butterflies, such as crawl, flutter, eggs and leaf.

- Write alliterative sentences relating to caterpillars and butterflies. Examples are:
  A curly crawling caterpillar nibbled a lovely lettuce leaf;
  A beautiful bouncing butterfly fluttered towards a gorgeous golden garden.
- Copy out the sentences on butterfly-shaped paper.
- Ask the children to imagine that they can change like a caterpillar changes into a butterfly. Write about what they would change into and why?
- Hold a puppet show. The children could use their butterfly and caterpillar puppets to create their own story.

Art and Design Technology

- Practise drawing, using butterflies as the subject.
- Paint giant butterflies and add sticky paper shapes to create symmetrical patterned wings.
- Sew symmetrical patterns onto binca fabric. Cut into butterfly shapes.
- Use different materials and threads to sew fabric caterpillars on a hessian background.
- Design and make a butterfly finger puppet or a caterpillar glove puppet.

Mathematics

- Investigate symmetry. Ask the children to match the shapes on one side of a butterfly-shaped piece of paper by drawing, cutting and sticking the shapes on to the other side.
- Look for evidence of symmetry in the environment, for example patterns on roofs, gates, flowers and insects.
- Investigate: Are all 2D shapes symmetrical?' Give the children a selection of giant paper shapes to fold, cut or draw in the lines of symmetry. Plot the results on a chart.
- Make a giant caterpillar number line, 1 to 20.

Science

- Compare the life cycle of a butterfly with the life cycles of other insects. Encourage the children to discuss the similarities and differences.
- Draw and label the parts of a butterfly. Ask the children to discuss the functions of the different parts.

Daedalus and Icarus

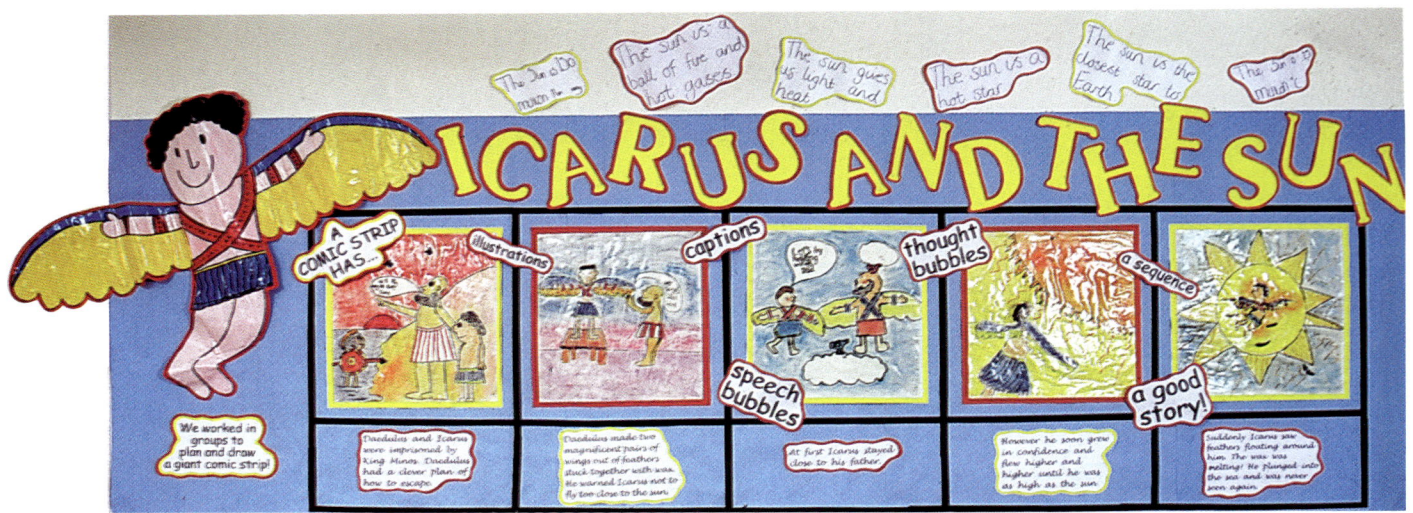

Literacy

- **Fiction:** 'Daedalus and Icarus' by Marcia Williams, *Greek Myths For Young Children*.
- Look at a variety of comic strip stories and identify common features such as illustrations, captions and speech bubbles.
- Create your own comic strip story based on 'Daedalus and Icarus'. Limit the strip to five frames.
- Make up anagrams linked to the story of Icarus. Ask a partner to unscramble the words.
- Write facts about the sun on sun-shaped paper or use them to create a fact sheet or leaflet about the sun.
- Write similes related to the sun, beginning, for example, 'As hot as …', 'As spiky as…'.
- Design a poster warning of the dangers of too much sun.
- Encourage the children to make up and write their own myth about the sun.

Poems and Rhymes

- 'Sunflakes' by Frank Asch, *Outdoor Poems* selected by Wendy Body.
- 'I Can't Take The Sun No More Man' by Linval Quinland, *Poems for the Very Young* selected by Michael Rosen.
- 'Summer Sun' by Robert Louis Stevenson, *A Child's Garden of Verses*.

Art and Design Technology

- Use chalk pastels to create suns.
- Draw a sun design on a polystyrene tile. Cover with paint using a roller and print as a repeating pattern onto fabric or paper.
- Use fabric dye to paint a sun onto calico. Use gold thread to stitch around the edge of the sun. Add a sprinkle of gold glitter to create a shimmering effect.
- Colour-mix hot colours and paint on sun-shaped paper.
- Make a clay sun tile. Spray or paint yellow, red and orange.
- Make batik sun pictures using melted wax.
- Design a labyrinth for the man-eating Minotaur.
- Design and make personalised sunglasses. The glasses must show something about the child, for example, a child who likes football could make a pair of glasses in the shape of footballs.

Science

- Investigate the effect of sunlight on plants by growing cress in different light and dark conditions.
- Investigate shadows by placing a cone or similar object on the playground in the sun. Draw around the shadow cone at hourly intervals during the day. Ask the children to observe the changes.

Geography

- Locate Greece and Athens on a world map.
- Find the Greek island of Crete where Daedalus and Icarus fled.
- Make a travel brochure advertising the main attractions in Greece or Crete.

Personal, Social and Health Education

- Discuss the issue of doing as you are told. Consider what happened to Icarus when he did not do as he was told.
- Ask the children to think about times when they have not done as they were told. What were the consequences? Why is it important to listen to adults?

Daffodils

Literacy

- **Poetry:** 'Daffodils' by William Wordsworth, *Outdoor Poems: Big Book* selected by Wendy Body.
- Discuss the line: 'I wandered lonely as a cloud'. What else might be considered as lonely? Ask the children to think of other ways of wandering alone, for example, 'I wandered lonely as a sailboat.'
- Find alternative words to suggest a crowd or host of daffodils. Subsitute them into the poem.
- Brainstorm other adjectives to replace 'fluttering' and 'dancing'.

from Daffodils

I wandered lonely as a cloud
That floats on high o'er vales and hills
When all at once I saw a crowd
A host of golden daffodils
Beside the lake
Beneath the trees
Fluttering and dancing in the breeze

William Wordsworth

- Substitute alternative words, lines and phrases to create your own version of the 'Daffodils' poem.
- Observe daffodils and brainstorm words to describe them. Use the words to write factual accounts, focusing on good sentence structure.
- Introduce to the children a fictitious character such as Dilly the Daffodil, a magical daffodil who has the power to grant wishes. Discuss story beginnings and settings, and use Dilly as a stimulus for encouraging children to write their own beginning to a story.

Poems and Rhymes

- 'A Spring Flower Riddle' by David Whitehead, *Scholastic Collections – Poetry* selected by Wes Magee.

Art and Design Technology

- Complete observational drawings and paintings of daffodils. Use watercolours or chalk pastels.
- Colour-mix as many shades of yellow as possible.
- Use fabric dye to paint daffodils on to calico.
- Paint a picture to illustrate Wordworth's poem 'Daffodils'.

Mathematics

- Count the number of petals on a daffodil. Count in 6s, make patterns of 6 and look at the 6-times table.
- Investigate how many different sums you can make using the numbers 1 to 6. For example, $3 + 4 = 7$, $6 - 3 = 3$, $2 \times 6 = 12$ and so on.

Science

- Undress a daffodil by taking apart a real daffodil. Stick each piece onto card and label the parts.
- Discuss the function of each part of the daffodil, such as petal, stem, stamen, pollen and so on.
- Plant and observe the growth of spring flowers. Investigate the conditions necessary for growth.

The Drop Goes Plop

Literacy

- **Fiction:** *The Drop Goes Plop* by Sam Godwin.
- Find other 'op' words that rhyme with plop and drop. Make simple rhyming sentences using 'op' words.
- Write a list of words used in the water cycle and order them alphabetically.
- Write a glossary of words relating to the water cycle.
- Make a wordsearch of words relating to the water cycle.
- Label a diagram of the water cycle using appropriate words (evaporation, water vapour, clouds, sun, precipitation, condensation).
- Find little words in the big word 'evaporation'.
- Write anagrams using water cycle words, for example, ldoucs (clouds), nsu (sun).
- Write your own explanation of the water cycle. The children could use their own choice of characters to retell the story.

- Ask the children to imagine that they have been evaporated by the sun and dropped as rain in a far away place. How would they feel? What did they see on their journey? Where did they land? Who did they meet? How did they get back?
- Write a class poem using Michael Rosen's poem 'The Sound of Water' as a stimulus.

Poems and Rhymes

- 'The Sound of Water' by Michael Rosen, *Don't Put Mustard in the Custard* by Michael Rosen.
- 'Water Cycle' by Noel Petty, *Scholastic Collections – Poetry* selected by Wes Magee.
- 'Beans' by Michael Rosen, *Michael Rosen's Book of Nonsense* by Michael Rosen.

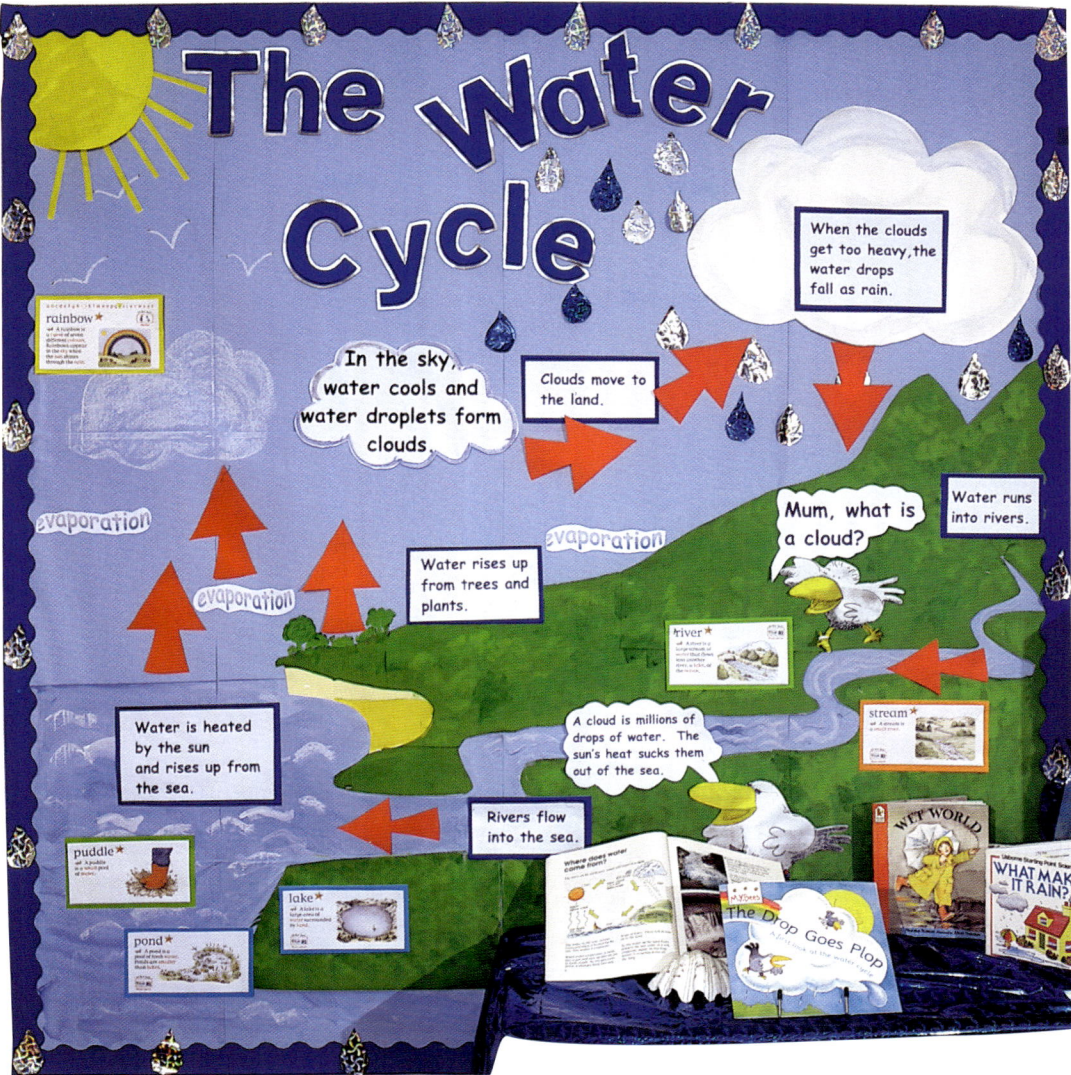

Art and Design Technology

- Use marbling inks to create a water effect and use as a background for collage work or cut into strips for weaving.
- Blend chalk pastels onto raindrop-shaped paper.
- Colour-mix blue, white and green to make the colours of water.
- Use drawing inks on wet paper to create watery patterns.

Mathematics

- Investigate water measures and capacity, for example, 'Is 1 litre of water enough to ... have a bath? brush your teeth? give a drink to an elephant?'

Science

- Investigate evaporation. Find a puddle in the playground. Chalk around the edge and visit the puddle at set times during the day. Find out and discuss what happens.
- Make a rain gauge. Collect and measure water over a period of a week. Plot your results on a graph.

Geography

- Identify oceans of the world and locate them on a globe or world map.
- Identify local rivers on a map. Follow them from their source to the sea.
- Talk about the countries of the world that suffer from drought. How do they manage? What could we do to help them? How would we feel if we had to suffer as they do?
- Make a plan of the journey of a drop of water from the clouds to the sea.

Elmer

Literacy

- **Fiction:** *Elmer* by David Mckee.
- Create a story map to retell the story of Elmer.
- Working in pairs, write questions relating to pictures from the text, for example, 'What is Elmer doing?' 'Why does Elmer want to run away?'
- List Elmer's colours and order them alphabetically.
- Put the letters of the word 'elephant' into alphabetical order.
- Make an elephant wordsearch, using words such as tusk, trunk, ivory and tail.
- Encourage the children to write their own adventure for Elmer.
- Plan an Elmer day parade, design and write invitations to the celebration.
- Write elephant facts on giant size elephant-shaped paper.
- Create a non-fiction zigzag book about elephants.

Poems and Rhymes

- 'The Blind Man and the Elephant' by John Godfrey Saxe, *The Oxford Treasury of Children's Poetry* selected by Michael Harrison and Chris Stuart-Clark.

Art and Design Technology

- Draw Elmer and use coloured pencils to create a patchwork background.
- Use coloured fabrics to create a giant patchwork collage of Elmer. Use newspaper to create a collage of a grey elephant.
- Colour-mix the colours of Elmer on elephant-shaped paper.
- Make small clay Elmers.
- Use oil pastels to design patterns on elephant-shaped paper for Elmer day.
- Design and make an elephant mask for the Elmer day parade.

Dance, Drama and Role Play

- Retell the story of Elmer through dance and drama. Use the following music for each stage of the story:
  – Happy Elmer dancing: 'Hippy, Hippy Shake' by the Swinging Blue Jeans, *The Swinging Blue Jeans 25 Greatest Hits*, (EMI Gold, 1998).
  – Sneaking to the jungle: 'Theme from Mission: Impossible' (Single) by Adam Clayton and Larry Mullen, (Mother).
  – Rolling in the berries: 'Shakin' all over' by Johnny Kidd & the Pirates, *Johnny Kidd & the Pirates 25 Greatest Hits*, (EMI Gold, 1998).
  – Elmer day celebrations: 'Celebration' by Kool & the Gang, *The Best of Kool & the Gang*, (Mercury).
- Re-enact one of Elmer's adventures or talk about a situation when the children made someone laugh.

Personal, Social and Health Education

- Discuss the meaning of 'showing your true colours' and 'standing out in a crowd'. Investigate the origins of these phrases.
- Ask the children to think about what makes them different. Do they think it is important to be the same as everyone else? Has anyone ever been made fun of because they are 'different'?

The Enormous Crocodile

Literacy

- **Fiction:** *The Enormous Crocodile* by Roald Dahl.
- Draw a story map and use speech bubbles to retell the story.
- Ask the children to create a list of words they can make using the letters in the title of the book, *The Enormous Crocodile*. Write them on crocodile-shaped paper.
- Write descriptive sentences about the Enormous Crocodile.
- Write factual words about crocodiles on open-mouthed crocodile heads. Include words such as camouflage, sharp, snappy, green scales, amphibian.
- Describe one of the Enormous Crocodile's clever tricks.
- Write your own clever trick to help the crocodile to capture children or teachers, or think of a clever trick to play on the Enormous Crocodile.
- Design 'Wanted' posters asking for the capture of the Enormous Crocodile.
- Write alliterative sentences about the Enormous Crocodile such as: 'The great, greedy, grumptious, green crocodile'; 'The horrid, hoggish, hungry, heavy crocodile'.
- Make up similes relating to the crocodile's teeth such as: 'His terrible, sharp teeth sparkled like knives in the sun.'
- Write letters from the other animals in the story to persuade the Enormous Crocodile to change his ways. The animals could suggest something kind that the crocodile could do for the children to say sorry for his evil behaviour.
- Create a display for the book corner entitled 'Snap up a Book!' Compose captions about books, such as: 'Books are exciting'; 'Books are fun'. Display the captions on open-mouthed crocodile heads.

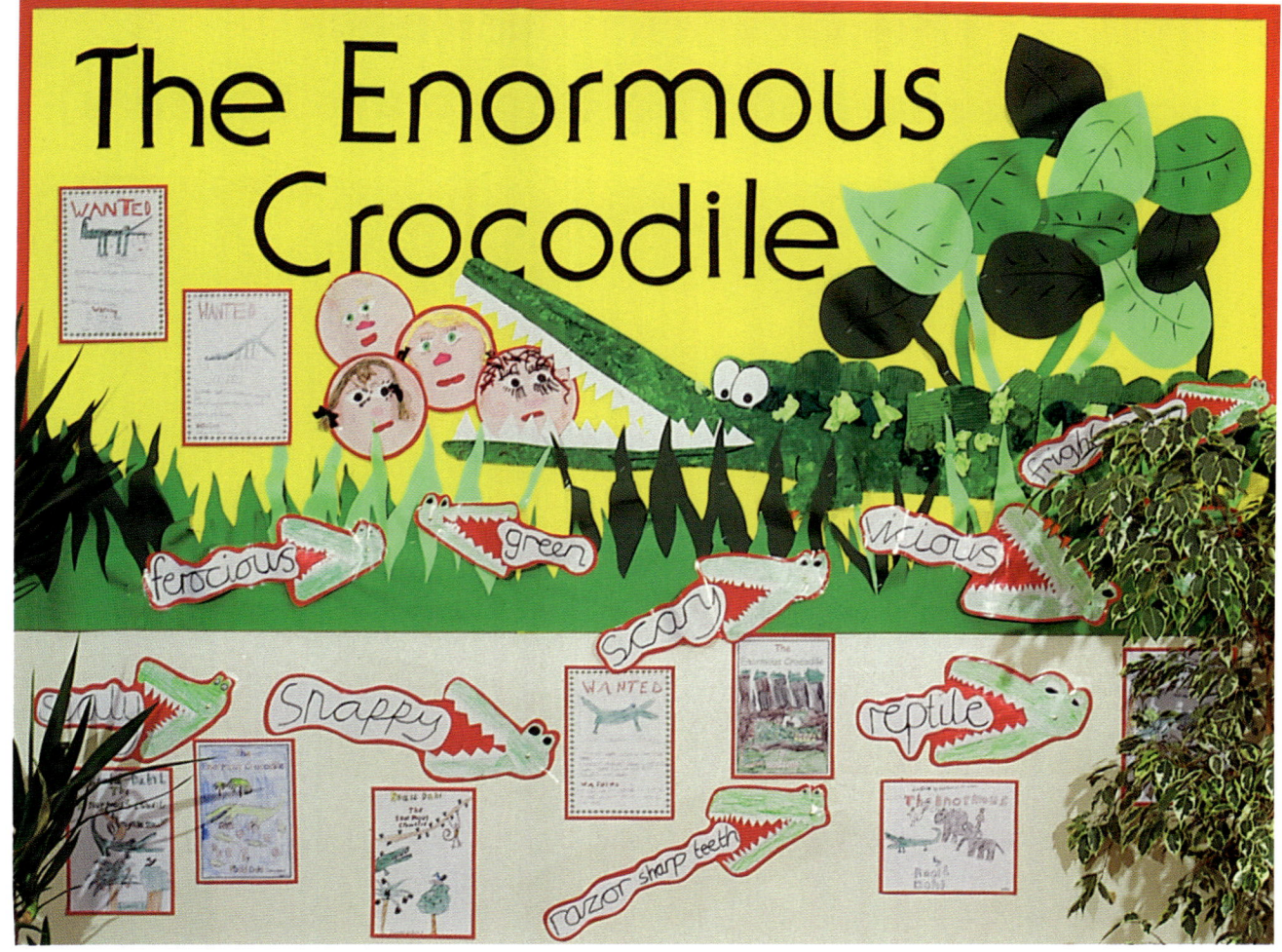

Art and Design Technology

- Make a giant collage crocodile using a variety of textiles and materials.
- Look carefully at the illustrations in *The Enormous Crocodile* and think of other ways the crocodile could hide himself. Paint pictures showing the crocodile using different types of camouflage.
- Design a new front cover for the book.
- Design and make a crocodile head with a hinged moving jaw.

Mathematics

- Make and use small crocodile measuring sticks for non-standard measuring activities.
- Make a crocodile hand puppet to play 'snap up a number'. Use the puppet for subtraction activities, for example, 'I have 6 sweets and the crocodile gobbles up 2 of them. How many are left?'
- Make 2 small snappy crocodiles from card and laminate them. Use these for bigger than (>), smaller than (<) activities. Work in pairs and give each pair of children a pile of numbers. Take turns to pick up two numbers and put them on the correct sides of the crocodile's mouth to show 'bigger than' or 'smaller than'.

Geography

- Locate Africa on a world map.
- Find out about the type of habitat in which crocodiles live.
- Draw a map of the Enormous Crocodile's journey from the river, through the jungle to the playground.

Dance, Drama and Role Play

- 'Hot-seat' the Enormous Crocodile and encourage the children to ask questions about his behaviour. Try to change his ways.
- Prepare a drama session in which the animals try to persuade the Enormous Crocodile to find a new diet of fish instead of children. Try to convince the crocodile to reform!

The Golden Tickets!
(from Charlie And The Chocolate Factory)

Literacy

- **Fiction:** 'The Golden Tickets!' Chapter 5 from *Charlie And The Chocolate Factory* by Roald Dahl.
- Ask the children to imagine that they found the last Golden Ticket. Describe how they felt, what they did and who they told first. Write their account in a golden ticket-shaped book.
- Write a persuasive letter to Willy Wonka explaining why they deserve to have the last Golden Ticket.
- Write your own 'Evening Bulletin' reporting on the five Golden Tickets. Report on the people who find the tickets and their reaction to their good fortune.
- Design and make your own chocolate bars. Think of a novel way to make people or children want to buy them.
- Write jingles such as 'this creamy, crunchy crocodile bar will snap your taste buds from afar!' to promote your new chocolate bar.
- Make a list of your favourite chocolate bars and put them in alphabetical order.
- Taste a variety of different chocolate bars and list adjectives that describe them.
- Write poems about chocolate, using the adjectives collected.
- Complete an author study of Roald Dahl. Find out information about him. Read and compare other Roald Dahl books.

Poems and Rhymes

- 'Chocolate Cake' by Michael Rosen, *Quick, Let's Get Out of Here* by Michael Rosen.
- 'Chocolate' by Michael Rosen, *Centrally Heated Knickers* by Michael Rosen.

Art and Design Technology

- Design and make your own brand of a giant chocolate bar using a variety of junk materials and papers.
- The Aztecs created the first chocolate drink. Make Aztec drinking chocolate and compare it with today's brands.
- The Aztecs drank chocolate from golden goblets. Encourage the children to create their own golden goblet designs using string patterns stuck on paper and sprayed gold.

Mathematics

- Survey favourite chocolate bars and record the results as a graph. Interpret the results.
- Estimate and measure the length and weight of different chocolate bars.

Information Technology

- The Aztecs were the first people to discover chocolate. Use the internet to research information about chocolate and the Aztecs.
- Use a word processing package to write an 'Evening Bulletin' report for the newspaper. Combine all the bulletins written by the children to make a newspaper.

Aztec Drinking Chocolate xocolatl

Method

1. Mix 2 teaspoons of cocoa with 4 teaspoons of water.
2. Stir it into a smooth paste.
3. Add a cup of cold water and a few drops of vanilla essence.
4. Whisk the mixture until it is foamy.
5. Add some ground black pepper.

Let the children sip the mixture to see if they like it.

Handa's Surprise

Literacy

- **Fiction:** *Handa's Surprise* by Eileen Browne.
- Cover the words of the story and ask the children to describe what is happening in each picture. Use this information to write the story in their own words and then compare their ideas with the actual text from the story.
- List the names of the fruits featured in the story and put them in alphabetical order.
- Work in groups to write and illustrate a 'fruity' alphabet.

- Taste the different fruits featured in the story and write a sentence to describe each piece of fruit, such as, 'a soft yellow banana', 'sweet juicy pineapple'. Create a poem using these ideas.
- Make a matching game using the fruits and the animals from the story. Make individual cards showing pictures of each fruit and each animal. Turn the cards face down on the table and ask the children to pick up two cards at a time. If they match, they keep the cards, for example, monkey and banana, ostrich and guava and so on.
- Using the pictures from the story, ask the children to imagine what the animals might be thinking or saying. Write these in speech bubbles or think bubbles.
- Ask the children to write their own definition of each fruit featured in the story and then use a dictionary to compare.
- Use the sense of taste, touch, smell and sight to create a class poem about a particular fruit.
- Write a recipe for a fruit salad using the fruits featured in the story.
- Write a book review for *Handa's Surprise*. Write it in pineapple-shaped books or other fruit-shaped books.

32

Art and Design Technology

- Make observational drawings and paintings of the fruits featured in the story. Colour-mix appropriate shades using paints or watercolour pencils.
- Make fruit prints to create repeated patterns and designs.
- Weave a basket shape using a variety of papers. Stick this on to a larger piece of paper and ask the children to draw or cut out different fruits from magazines to make a basket of fruit collage.
- Use salt dough to make 3D fruits.
- Design and make a basket to protect Handa's fruit from the animals.
- Design, make and serve a recipe for an exotic fruit salad.

Mathematics

- Cut a variety of fruits into different fractions, for example, halves and quarters. Repeat using fruit-shaped paper which they cut into the appropriate fractions to record their work.
- Make a fraction game based on halves and quarters. Draw a half or a quarter of a fruit onto a piece of card. Write the corresponding fraction on another piece of card. Ask the children to match the two correctly.
- Weigh different fruits using non-standard measures. Ask the children to estimate and discover how many tangerines balance a pineapple, how many bananas balance an avocado and so on.
- Use standard weight to estimate and weigh the different fruits featured in the story. Order the fruits according to their weight.

Science

- Investigate different ways of keeping fruit fresh. Give each group of children a banana and ask them to find a way of keeping it fresh for a set period of time. For example, the children might put the banana in the refrigerator, wrap it in foil, put it in a container and so on.
- Blindfold the children and ask them to use different senses to guess a variety of different fruits. Discuss with the children which of the senses they found most useful. Did it vary from fruit to fruit?

Hurry, Santa!

Literacy

- **Fiction:** *Hurry, Santa!* by Julie Sykes.
- Predict what might be in the present for Santa at the end of the story. List other appropriate presents to give to Santa at Christmas.
- Draw a story plan of Santa's adventure in *Hurry, Santa!*
- Draw a cartoon or comic strip to retell the story. Use speech bubbles to highlight what Santa and the animals might be saying.
- Write an account of an occasion when you were late and had to hurry to get somewhere, just as Santa did.
- Write sentences to describe Santa. Focus on his characteristics, for example, 'Santa wears a red coat and has a fat tummy', 'He carries a big heavy sack and has a white fluffy beard.'

- Ask the children to write a letter to Santa telling him what they would like for Christmas. Ask them to tell Santa why they think they should receive these presents. For example, 'Dear Santa, Please may I have a toy car and a train set? I have been good all year and I keep my room really tidy ... .'
- Write, in alphabetical order, a Christmas list of ten things they would like Santa to leave in their stocking on Christmas morning.
- Write a Christmas acrostic using the letters in 'Santa'.
- Read a variety of different stories about Santa. Discuss with the children the sorts of adventures Santa could have on Christmas Eve. Focus on a story setting, characters, the problem and the solution.
- Ask the children to write their own Santa adventure or write an alternative ending to the story *Hurry, Santa!*

Poems and Rhymes

- 'Letters to Santa' by Jacqueline Brown, *Another First Poetry Book* selected by John Foster.
- 'The Snow Lies White' Anon, *Poems for Christmas* selected by Jill Bennett.
- 'The Waiting Game' by John Mole in *Poems for Christmas* selected by Jill Bennett.

Art and Design Technology

- Draw or paint pictures of Santa.
- Create a large collage Santa from a variety of paper and materials.
- Design and make a 3D sleigh for Santa using recycled materials.

- Make Santa puppets or masks.
- Design and make an Advent Calendar to help Santa with his countdown to Christmas.
- Design and make a Christmas decoration.
- Design and make a Christmas clock for Santa.
- Make Santa-face biscuits.

Mathematics

- Sort and classify a variety of 3D parcels according to their shape (for example, cube, cuboid, sphere, cylinder, prism and pyramid).
- Weigh Santa's parcels and put them in order, from heaviest to lightest.
- Set time problems for Santa. For example, 'Santa is half an hour late for each delivery. He arrived at 12.30pm, 2pm and 4.30pm. Write down the correct time that he should have arrived.'

Information Technology

- Use a drawing package to design Christmas cards or draw Santa pictures.
- Use a word processing package to sort sentences according to whether they are true or false statements about Santa, or about events in the story *Hurry, Santa!*
- E-mail a message or Christmas list to Santa.
- Use the internet to find out about St Nicholas.

In the Garden

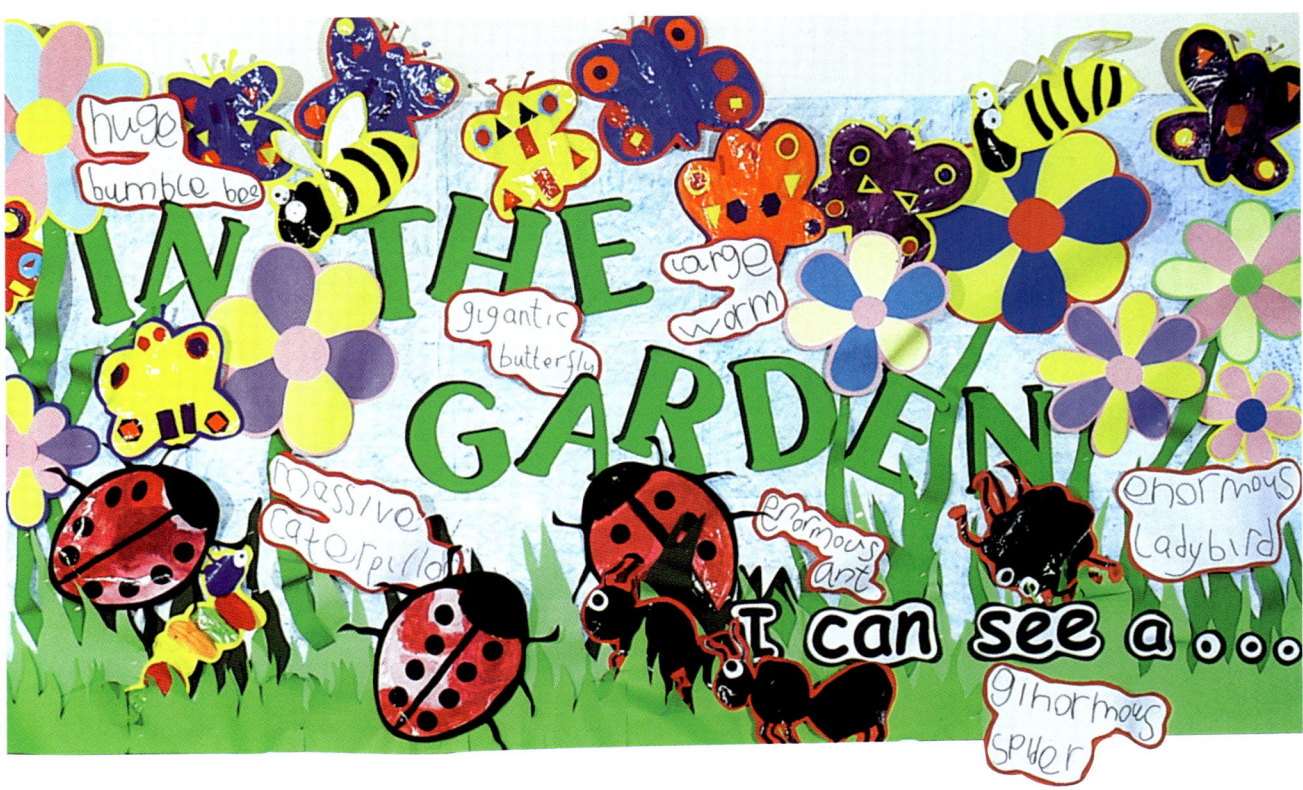

Literacy

- **Fiction:** *In the Garden* by Richard Powell.
- Play I Spy with things that you might expect to find in the garden.
- Ask the children to write descriptively about the things they would find in the garden. Encourage the use of a variety of words that mean the same as 'big', for example, an enormous bee, a giant flower, a gigantic ladybird.
- Make a big alphabet book based on things in the garden, such as A is for ant, B is for butterfly ... Z is for zigzag path.
- Use alliterative words and phrases to describe mini-beasts found in the garden, such as angry ants, beautiful butterflies and so on.
- Ask the children to make their own In the Garden 'flip the flap' book based on the things they might find in their own back garden.
- Encourage the children to write a fact file about insects. Working in groups, each member could research facts about one particular insect. The children can then collate their work and put it into alphabetical order.
- Write a rhyming book about an insect found in the garden, for example, a ladybird. Follow a question and answer format such as:

Ladybird, ladybird what do you see?
I see a big caterpillar crawling towards me.

Poems and Rhymes

- 'I'm an Ant' by Pam Brewster, *Mini Beasties* selected by Michael Rosen.
- 'Hey, Bug!' by Lilian Moore, *Mini Beasties* selected by Michael Rosen.

Art and Design Technology

- Paint giant insects and bugs found in the garden.
- Make observational drawings of garden flowers.
- Use card, paper and paint to make insect masks.
- Make a clay tile of a mini-beast.
- Design and make a giant insect using a variety of junk materials.
- Design and make a mini-spring garden.

Geography

- Ask the children to draw a plan of their garden at home. (If they do not have a garden, they could draw a plan of the school's gardens or grounds.)
- Draw a giant grid on the playground. Place garden items on the grid and ask the children to identify the appropriate grid references.

Science

- Go on a mini-beast hunt in the school grounds to find and observe as many different insects as possible.
- Draw and label the parts of different insects.
- Encourage the children to create their own key to help classify the insects.
- Discuss the conditions necessary for growth. Investigate the best conditions for the growth of cress or sweet peas. Put the seeds in different places around the school and monitor their progress over several weeks.
- Plant vegetables and flowers in the school garden in pots.

Information Technology

- Use the internet to find facts about different insects for the insect fact file (see Literacy activity).
- Transform a Roamer or Pixie into a giant insect and take it on an adventure in the garden. Program the toy to move to different landmarks.

The Jolly Postman

Literacy

- **Fiction:** *The Jolly Postman or Other People's Letters* by Janet and Allan Ahlberg.
- Identify the nursery rhyme and fairy tale characters that the Jolly Postman delivers letters to on his journey. For example, The Three Bears.
- Learn and recite the rhymes visited in the story such as 'The Grand Old Duke of York', 'Tom, Tom the Piper's Son' and 'Bye Baby Bunting'.
- Make up a new postal address for a character featured in the story. Write the address on a brightly coloured envelope, for example, Wicked Witch, Candy Cottage, Wicked Woods.
- Ask the children to think of alliterative sentences relating to the characters in the story, for example, 'The Jolly Postman went to visit the Wicked Witch', 'He had a letter for bouncy Baby Bear.'
- Write an order from Hobgoblin Supplies. List the items the witch might order and why she needs them, for example, 'I would like to order a pair of black Halloween boots size 18 as I have accidentally turned my existing pair into two fat green frogs.'
- Write a recipe for making Little Boy Pie Mix from Hobgoblin Supplies.
- Ask the children to design a birthday card for Goldilocks and write their own verse inside.
- Write a list of party foods for Goldilock's birthday party or the Jolly Postman's tea party. Put them in alphabetical order.
- Write a letter to one of the characters in the story. As a stimulus, give the children a letter from the characters, for example, a giant's postcard or a witch's letter, which they can reply to.
    - Write a letter to the witch on green paper and suggest things to buy from the catalogue or tell her how to be a kind witch.
    - Write a postcard to the giant. Draw pictures of where they live on the postcard and tell the giant about themselves and the things they do in their 'home town'.
- Ask the children to write their own *The Jolly Postman* story. Ask the children to visit three of the characters in the story. What would they deliver? What would they say to the different characters?
- Read some of the fairy tales in *The Jolly Postman* story, for example, 'Hansel and Gretel', 'The Three Bears' and 'Little Red Riding Hood'.

Art and Design Technology

- Design a new stamp for each of the character's letters featured in the story.
- Design and make an envelope to send a letter to one of the story characters.
- Draw pictures of the Jolly Postman's bicycle.
- Make collage houses for each of the characters in the story.
- Make some jelly and party food for Goldilock's party or the Jolly Postman's tea party.

Mathematics

- Measure the length of a variety of envelopes using standard and non-standard measures. Record the measures, for example, 'My envelope is 6 cubes long', 'My envelope is 2 pencils long', 'My envelope is 6 centimetres long'.
- Look at different stamps on old envelopes. Sort the stamps according to size, colour, shape and value.
- Look at the times and dates shown on post marks. Put them in order.
- Calculate the cost of party food for Goldilock's birthday party. What can the children buy for 20p, 50p, £1, £5?
- Weigh a variety of the postman's letters, packages and parcels using standard and non-standard measures.

Information Technology

- Use a Roamer or Pixie to deliver letters to various characters featured in the story. Place large pictures of the characters or their houses around the room and program the Roamer or Pixie so that it visits the characters in the same order as they appear in the story.
- Use a drawing package to design a birthday card for Goldilocks or create an invitation for the Jolly Postman's tea party.
- Send an e-mail to a character from the story. Compare e-mails to letters – discuss similarities and differences.

Geography

- Draw a map of the Jolly Postman's journey featured in the story.
- Look at the local environment and identify a number of features that you could draw on a postcard that would tell a friend about the place where you live.

The Kind Christmas Tree

The Kind Christmas Tree

The summer was over. Each morning when little bird woke up, the air was cold and crisp. Sometimes frost sparkled on the grass until the autumn sun melted it away. The little bird knew that winter would soon be here.

He watched the other birds getting ready to fly away to a warmer country over the sea. They would stay there until the winter was over. But the little bird wasn't strong enough to fly so far. He would need to find a new home, somewhere away from the cold winds and the snow.

So early one morning he began to look for a winter home. He flew for a long time until he came to a forest. 'This would be a good place to stay for the winter', he said. 'I'll find the biggest, strongest tree in the whole forest, and spend the winter hiding among the leaves.'

The tallest tree of all was a strong oak tree. Perching on a branch the little bird asked, very politely, if he could shelter among the leaves until spring came.

The oak tree shook his thick leaves. 'Certainly not! Be off with you!' And although the little bird promised that he wouldn't eat a single acorn, the oak tree still said 'No'.

On the little bird flew, until he came to a birch tree with pretty silvery bark. Perching on a branch he asked, very politely, if he could shelter amongst the leaves until spring came.

The birch tree shook his silvery green leaves. 'Certainly not! I'm not sharing with anyone. Away you go!' And although the bird said that he was so small that he would hardly take up any room at all, the birch tree still said 'No'.

So the bird flew away until he came to a willow tree bending his long branches over a stream. Perching on a branch he asked, very politely, if he could spend the winter among the leaves.

The willow rustled his leaves crossly. 'No, you can't stay here, I'd rather be on my own. Fly away, little bird!' And although the little bird said he would be so quiet the willow tree wouldn't know he was there, still the answer was 'No'.

Sadly, the little bird flew away again. It was almost dark when he came to the very middle of the forest. And there, growing amongst the tall trees was a tiny Christmas tree. Very politely, the little bird asked if he could shelter among the Christmas tree's branches for the winter.

'Certainly you can', said the kind Christmas tree. 'I don't have thick leaves like the oak tree or the birch tree or the willow tree, but you're welcome to stay with me. I'll give you what shelter I can.'

Happy at last, the little bird settled down. Very soon winter came. Each day grew colder and darker, and the sun never shone. Then the snow came, falling from a grey sky in a blizzard of snowflakes. An icy wind blew through the forest. It blew all the leaves off the big, strong oak tree. It blew all the leaves off the pretty silver birch tree. It blew all the leaves off the bending willow tree. Their branches were bare. Not a single leaf was left.

But the wind didn't blow the fine green needles off the Christmas tree. It was the only tree in the forest to stay green all through the winter.

And the little bird was able to shelter safely among the branches of the kind Christmas tree until spring came again.

Anne English

Literacy

- **Fiction:** *The Kind Christmas Tree* by Anne English.
- Make a list of words to describe the behaviour of the kind Christmas tree. Ask the children to put the words in alphabetical order, for example, caring, considerate, friendly, gentle, helpful. Write the words on tree-shaped paper.
- Provide a selection of possible answers to questions relating to the story. The children have to think of the question that would match the answer.
- Find little words in 'Christmas tree', for example ('is', 'it', 'has', 'miss').
- Make a large picture book that tells the story of the kind Christmas tree. Discuss with the children the idea of being an illustrator and how important it is that the pictures tell the story. Add speech bubbles to the pictures and ask the children to write what they think the characters would be saying.
- Write the back cover blurb to put on the back of the picture book.
- Write a letter to the kind Christmas tree or the nasty oak tree, telling them what you thought about their behaviour towards the little bird.
- Write a 'thank you' card from the little bird to the Christmas tree expressing its gratitude and appreciation for allowing it to stay in his branches through the winter.
- Ask the children to write their own version of the kind Christmas tree story. They could use a different bird or animal and three different types of tree.
- Discuss facts about Christmas trees with the children, for example, where they originate, why they don't lose their leaves and so on. Ask the children to write facts about Christmas trees on Christmas tree-shaped paper.

Art and Design Technology

- Colour-mix shades of green. Hand-print the greens onto paper and cut them out. Use to create a giant Christmas tree.
- Make 3D Christmas trees out of paper or card.
- Illustrate the story of the kind Christmas tree. Use the pictures to make the large picture book. (See Literacy.)
- Look at the work of artist Paul Klee and paint Christmas trees in the same style.
- Design and make a Christmas decoration for the tree. Use a selection of card, foil, paper, tinsel, glitter, wire and string.
- Make and paint salt dough Christmas tree decorations.
- Make Christmas tree-shaped biscuits. Cover with green icing and decorate with small sweets.

Leaping Frogs

Literacy

- **Non-fiction:** *Leaping Frogs:* Big Book by Melvin Berger.
- Write simple sentences, beginning with a capital letter and ending with a full stop, giving a fact about frogs, for example 'A frog has webbed feet', 'A frog has round ears'.
- Look at other non fiction books about frogs. Discuss the different features and uses of the contents, index and glossary. Work in groups to find examples of contents, index and glossary pages.
- Write a Fact File about frogs, describing a frog's movements, habitat, food and appearance. Include a contents, glossary and index page.
- Give the children questions which they have to answer using their knowledge of frogs or give the children the answers and ask them to create the questions.
- Write a diary about life as a frog starting from when it is frogspawn through to being a fully-grown frog.
- **Fiction:** *Frog in the Throat* by Martin Waddell. Make up a different ending to the story to suggest a way of getting the frog out of the Baby Giraffe's throat.
- Discuss what the term 'Frog in the Throat' means. List the different ways that the giraffe tried to remove it in the story.
- Write alliterative frog sentences or phrases, such as: 'A friendly frog fried fruit on Friday'.
- Write rhyming sentences about 'My frog', for example, 'My frog can leap in his sleep', 'My frog can croak and tell a joke'.
- Ask the children to work in small groups and sort books into fiction and non-fiction. Ask them to report on the reasons for their decisions.

Poems and Rhymes

- 'The Frog's Lament' by Aileen Fisher, *A First Poetry Book* selected by John Foster.
- 'Porwigles' by Julie Holder, *A First Poetry Book* selected by John Foster.

Art and Design Technology

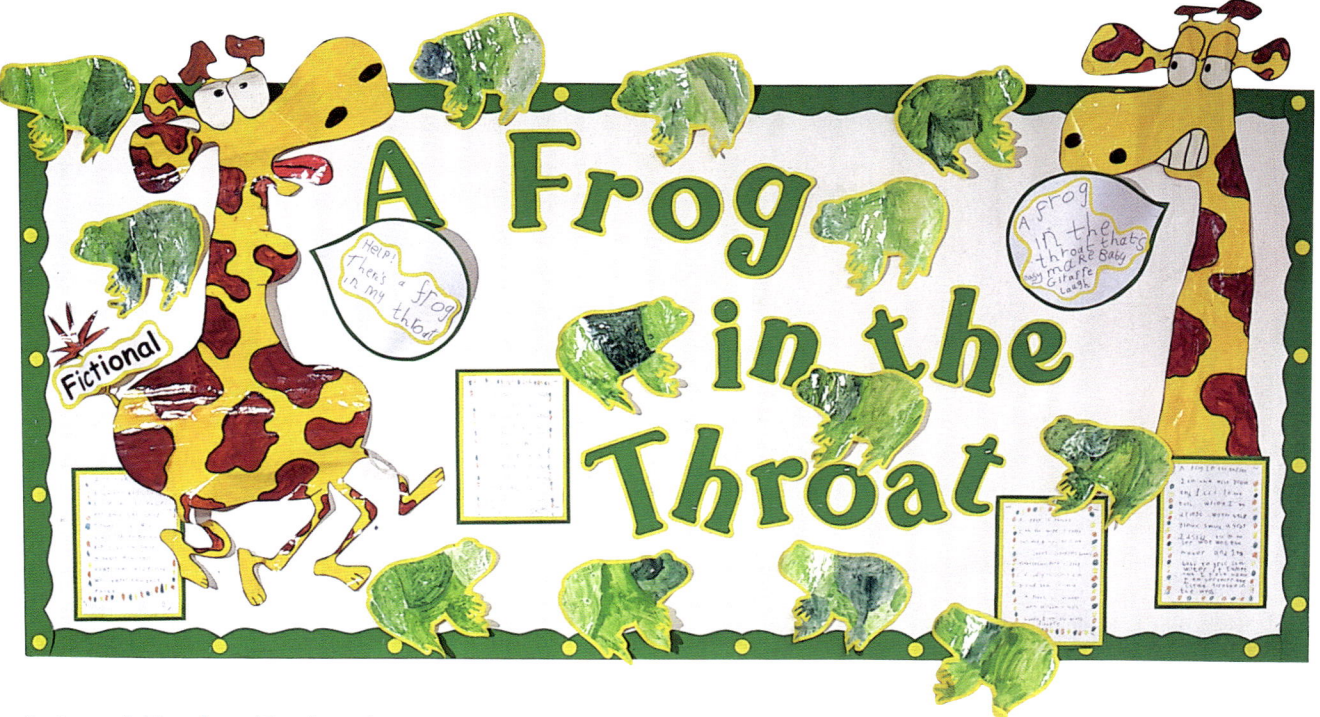

- Colour-mix shades of green and paint onto green frog-shaped paper.
- Make collage frog masks using green sticky paper.
- Sew bean-filled frogs using felt.
- Model the life cycle of a frog using clay.

Mathematics

- Create a large 100 square grid for the children to practise jumping on and back in 1s, 2s, 5s and 10s. The children could wear their frog masks for this activity.
- Make giant lily-pads and number them 1 to 10. Ask the children to investigate how many sums they can make using the lily-pad numbers.
- Put two lily pads one metre apart. Ask the children if they can jump as long as one metre, more than one metre or less than one metre. Plot the results. Ask the children to estimate and record how far they can jump.

Science

- Research the life cycle of a frog by looking at frogspawn and recording observed changes. Visit a pond to do some pond dipping.
- Research other amphibians and record similarities and differences in their appearance and behaviour, for example, compare frogs and crocodiles.
- Make a poster to emphasise the importance of keeping a pond area clean and safe for frogs and other wildlife.

Dance, Drama and Role Play

- Dance like frogs to:

  – 'Jump' by the Pointer Sisters, *The Pointer Sisters Greatest Hits*, (Camden).
  – 'It's Oh So Quiet' (Single) by Bjork, (One Little Indian).

- Practise a dance sequence in which the children mimic the quick darting actions of tadpoles. Intersperse the quick movements with slow movements.
- Practise a dance sequence in which the children mimic frog actions, such as leaping, jumping, catching flies and swimming. Focus on the use of legs and arms and include moments of stillness.
- Create a group dance which includes all the different stages of a frog's life cycle. Perform them in their correct order.

The Little Red Hen

Literacy

- **Fiction:** *The Little Red Hen* by Michael Foreman.
- Discuss the behaviour of the characters in the story. Was the little red hen right not to share her bread?
- Draw a story map to illustrate the activities of the little red hen.
- Retell the story in your own words modelling the story structure of the book.
- Compare different versions of *The Little Red Hen* story, such as: *Little Red Hen* by Ronne P Randall, *The Little Red Hen and the Ear of Wheat* by Mary Finch and *The Little Red Hen* by Margot Zemach.
- Write a different ending to *The Little Red Hen* story.
- Create speech bubbles for the characters in the text using the pictures from the story. What do you think each character might be saying?
- Write invitations from the little red hen to her new friends asking them to come for tea.
- Compose questions and answers relating to the story. Swop them with a partner.
- Write a recipe booklet for making bread on hen-shaped paper.

Poems and Rhymes

- 'Bread' by H E Wilkinson, *The Book of 1000 Poems* selected by J Murray Macbain.
- 'Catch them if you can!' by Judith Nicholls, *An Orange Poetry Paintbox* selected by John Foster.
- 'Harvest' by Jean Kenward, *A Blue Poetry Paintbox* selected by John Foster.

Art and Design Technology

- Make small loaves of bread out of salt dough.
- Colour-mix circles of red and yellow to represent the colours of the little red hen.
- Paint and collage the little red hen using shades of red and yellow. Collage tissue paper feathers.
- Hand-print shades of red and yellow. Cut each print out individually and use these to build up a large picture of the little red hen.
- Follow a recipe to bake bread.
- Design and make a bag or trolley to help the little red hen to carry her wheat, flour and loaves of bread.

Mathematics

- Investigate how many cubes balance one or two loaves or slices of bread.
- Use standard measures to weigh the ingredients for baking bread.
- Work out the ingredients required for making two loaves of bread or half a loaf of bread.
- Collect data about favourite types of bread and make a tally, pictogram or block graph to illustrate the results.

Science

- Set up a 'Yeast Feast' experiment to show how the action of sugar, yeast and warm water creates enough carbon dioxide to blow up a balloon.
- Find different ways to move a bag of flour.
- Investigate, discuss and identify the changes which occur in the bread making process, such as wheat to flour, flour to dough and dough to bread.

Geography

- Draw a map of the little red hen's journey and label all the places she visits.
- Look at different types of bread from around the world and locate the countries on a map of the world.

Dance, Drama and Role Play

- Role play one of the characters from the story. Hot-seat the character and encourage the children to ask questions based on the text.
- Organise the children into groups and set them a problem to solve: 'Some bread is left over. Which of the three animals can give the most convincing reason for why they were unable to help the little red hen?'

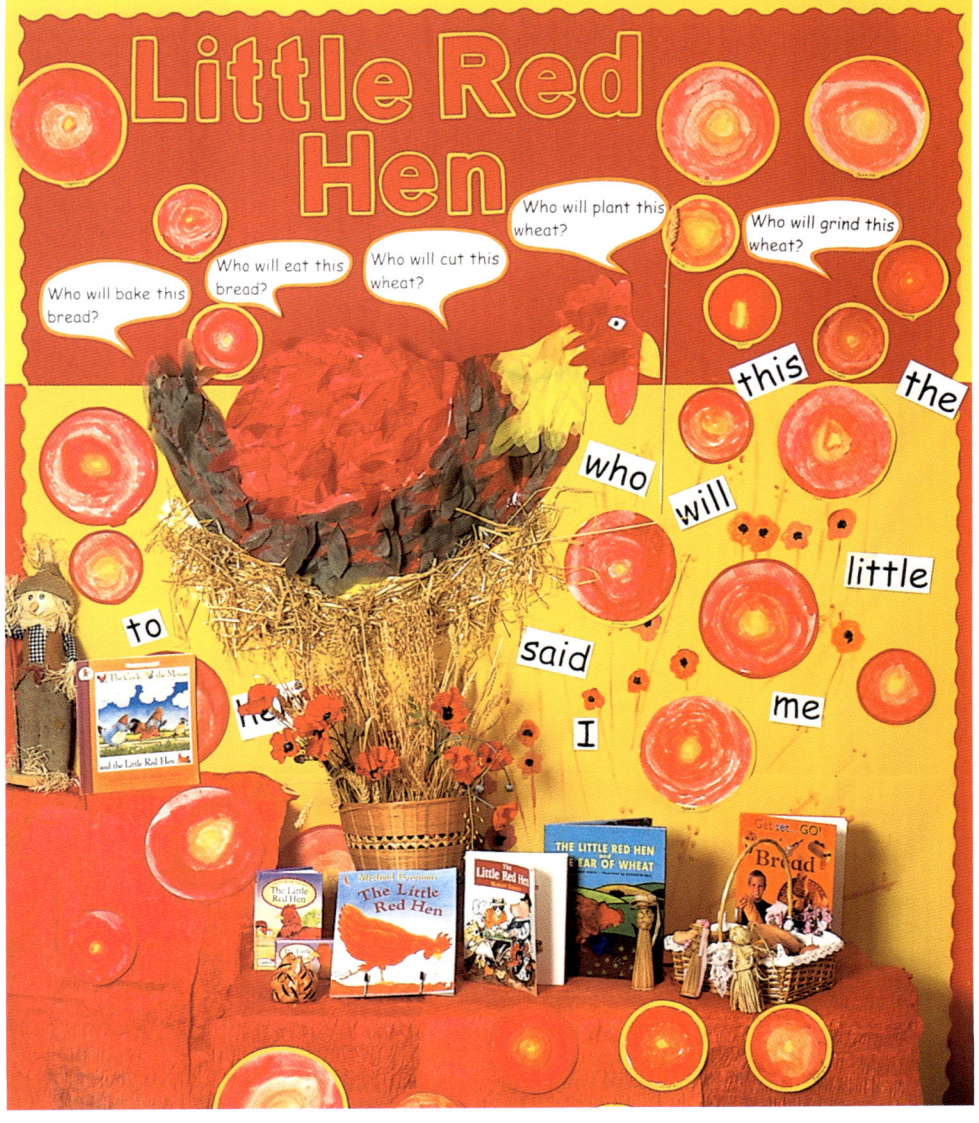

The Magic Bicycle

Literacy

- **Fiction:** *The Magic Bicycle* by Brian Patten.
- Draw a story map of Danny's journey on the magic bicycle.
- Invent new spells for Danny's bike that the witch might have created.
- Write postcards from Danny, from each of the different countries he visits around the world. These could be displayed on a world map.
- Find words that rhyme with 'bike'. Identify the rhyming words in the story and find other words that rhyme with them.
- Use a dictionary to find out the meanings of unusual words in the story, such as 'bazaar' and 'bedouin'.
- Write a different ending to the story.
- Ask the children to write about their own magic bicycle adventure. Where would their bike take them? Write their story on bicycle-shaped paper.
- Make a poster outlining the safety rules that bike-riders should follow.

Poems and Rhymes

- 'A Spider Bought a Bicycle' by Phyllis Kingsbury, *A Spider Bought a Bicycle* selected by Michael Rosen.
- 'Cycling down the street to meet my friend John' by Gareth Owen, *Scholastic Collections – Poetry* selected by Wes Magee.
- 'Downhill' by Sheila Simmons, *Another First Poetry Book* selected by John Foster.

Art and Design Technology

- Print wheel patterns or make tyre prints on circular paper.
- Paint colour wheels showing primary and secondary colours.
- Make observational drawings of the children's own bicycles.
- Paint and draw some of the famous landmarks featured in the story.
- Create paper collage bicycle frames and sew simple wheel spokes using coloured threads.
- Weave different coloured wool onto card wheels.
- Design and make a drink holder for Danny's magic bicycle.

Science

- Investigate the forces used when riding a bicycle. What do we pull or push on a bicycle and what happens as a result of these actions?
- Collect items from around school that require a push or pull.
- Cut out items from magazines and catalogues and sort them into those that require pushing and pulling, for example, a lawnmower, a pair of curtains and so on.

Information Technology

- Use the internet to research the countries identified in the story. Make a class 'Fact File' based on the research.

Geography

- Locate the countries featured in the story on a world map and plot the route taken by Danny, as shown at the front of the book.
- Plot the landmarks featured in the story, such as Ben Nevis, Tower Bridge, the Eiffel Tower and the Pyrenees.
- Find out about a famous landmark featured in the story. Write up the results of the research.

Mrs Armitage on Wheels

Literacy

- **Fiction:** *Mrs Armitage on Wheels* by Quentin Blake.
- Consider where Mrs Armitage may have been going on her bike. Make a list of suggested destinations.
- Suggest alternative ways of providing Mrs Armitage's bike with extra oomph.
- Devise a cloze procedure from *Mrs Armitage on Wheels*. Ask the children to fill in the missing words.
- Practise spelling common 'w' words used in the story.
- Spell and sequence the days of the week.
- Describe Mrs Armitage's character. Brainstorm words to describe her, for example inventive, practical, fussy and eccentric.

- Ask the children to think about words with sounds that resemble Mrs Armitage's actions throughout the story, for example: washing her hands – splish, splash, splosh; eating a snack – crunch, munch, gulp.
- Using pictures from the story, draw speech bubbles and write in what the characters might be saying.
- Ask the children to list the items which they think Mrs Armitage might need on her roller skates, for example rocket boosters and a lunch box. Draw these items on a large paper roller skate and cover each one with a paper flap that can be lifted. Decorate the whole skate in bright colours.
- Write a sequel to the story using the same story structure but based on 'What these roller skates need is ... .'
- Research information about the author, Quentin Blake. Read and compare *Mrs Armitage on Wheels* with other books by Quentin Blake such as *Mrs Armitage and the Big Wave*, *Zagazoo* and *Fantastic Daisy Artichoke*.

Art and Design Technology

- Draw Mrs Armitage's bicycle in the style of Quentin Blake.
- Paint colour wheels showing primary and secondary colours.
- Design bunting for Mrs Armitage's bicycle.
- Design a pair of roller skates for Mrs Armitage.
- Design and make a skateboard or other crazy vehicle with wheels for Mrs Armitage.
- Plan and make a healthy snack for Mrs Armitage to take on her journey.
- Design and make a new seat for Mrs Armitage's dog, Breakspear.

Mathematics

- Count in 2s, for example, 1 bicycle has 2 wheels, 2 bicycles have 4 wheels, and so on.
- Conduct a bicycle survey. Collect data about the colours of the children's bikes or the favourite places where they like to ride their bikes. Record data on a tally chart and block graph.
- Sequence the events in Mrs Armitage's day – getting up, having breakfast, lunch time. Draw clock faces with suggested times for these events.

Science

- Investigate the use of wind power as used by Mrs Armitage to give her bike more oomph. In small groups, make a land yacht using a variety of materials to make sails, such as cotton fabric, plastic, paper and card. Predict and test which material makes the best sail and moves the land yacht the furthest.
- Investigate how well roller skates move on different surfaces. Introduce the term 'friction' and find out which surface provides the most friction.
- Discuss the importance of exercise and healthy eating.

Dance, Drama and Role Play

- Invite Mrs Armitage to visit the classroom (the teacher can role play the character). Mrs Armitage arrives in a very distressed state because she has lost Breakspear, her dog. Encourage the children to help Mrs Armitage look for him and suggest places he could be hiding related to the places visited in the story.
- 'Hot-seat' Mrs Armitage and ask questions that have been prepared prior to the visit, for example, 'How old is Breakspear? What is your favourite food or piece of music? Where were you going?'

Mrs Jolly's Brolly

Literacy

- **Fiction:** *Mrs Jolly's Brolly* by Dick King-Smith.
- Ask the children to imagine they have found a magic umbrella like Mrs Jolly's brolly. Where would it take them? What would they see and do? Ask the children to write creatively about their adventure.
- Write a rhyming spell for Mrs Jolly's brolly to make them fly to the sky or bring them back down to earth again.
- Find words with 'y' endings, such as jolly, brolly, holly, Molly, Polly, silly and dilly.
- Discuss the use of the apostrophe in the title *Mrs Jolly's Brolly*. Ask the children to make up similar titles using an apostrophe in the same way, for example 'Polly's Shoes' and 'Tommy's Basketball'.
- Find stormy weather words that end in 'ed'. Add other 'ed' words to your list.
- Write an invitation to invite Mrs Jolly to the Witches' Annual Reunion Party.
- Design a poster advertising the Great Hot-Air Balloon Race.
- Ask the children to imagine they are a reporter and have seen Mrs Jolly flying above their house. Ask them to write an article for the local newspaper explaining what they saw, and to think of a snappy headline that will help sell the newspaper.

Art and Design Technology

- Design your own magic umbrella pattern using paint or watercolour pencils.
- Practise observational drawings of a closed umbrella, focusing on line.
- Ask the children to look carefully at part of an umbrella and draw what they see. Use this pattern for threadwork design.
- Ask the children to design a hot-air balloon to enter the Great Hot-Air Balloon Race.
- Make a hot-air balloon by covering a balloon with papier mâché and hanging a small woven basket beneath.

Science

- Set up an investigation to discover which fabrics are waterproof. Record and discuss the results.
- Make a simple rain gauge and collect rainwater over a period of time. Plot the results on a graph.

Information Technology

- Draw a table or a chart to record the amount of rainfall collected for each rainy day during a week.
- Use a microphone, tape recorder and video camera, to record a news report telling of Mrs Jolly's success at winning the Great Hot-Air Balloon Race.

Geography

- Ask the children to draw an imaginary map of Mrs Jolly's journey as seen from above. What could she see?
- Ask the children to draw a bird's eye view of their own bedroom, the classroom or the school grounds.

Oliver's Vegetables

Literacy

- **Fiction:** *Oliver's Vegetables* by Vivian French.
- Make a 'story wheel' to retell and sequence the story of *Oliver's Vegetables* pictorially. Ask the children to write the days of the week on each section of the wheel.
- Present a selection of jumbled sentences for each day of Oliver's week. Ask the children to put them in the correct order, for example, 'On Monday Oliver had carrots for lunch.'
- Retell the story using different vegetables for each day of the week.
- Provide a list of fruit and vegetables and ask the children to put them in alphabetical order.
- Make a fruit and vegetable 'Alphabet Book'.
- Create fruit and vegetable anagrams and give them to a friend to solve.
- Write a letter to Grandpa to say 'thank you' for all the lovely vegetables Oliver had in the week and to invite Grandpa to visit.
- Write sentences listing what Oliver might feed Grandpa for a week's visit, for example, 'On Monday I'll give Grandpa a jam sandwich', 'On Tuesday for supper I'll give Grandpa spaghetti.'
- Prepare a variety of vegetables for tasting. Ask the children to describe how they look, taste and smell. Write descriptions on vegetable-shaped paper.
- Invent a healthy eating quiz with questions such as: Which foods provide us with vitamins? protein? carbohydrates?

Poems and Rhymes

- 'Enough' by Michelle Magorian, *Another First Poetry Book* selected by John Foster.
- 'The Meal' by Karla Kuskin, *A Packet of Poems* selected by Jill Bennett.
- 'Harvest Festival' by Irene Yeats, *A Blue Poetry Paintbox* selected by John Foster.

Art and Design Technology

- Provide a selection of real fruit and vegetables. Ask the children to design their own funny fruit and vegetable faces in the style of Arcimboldo. Copy the design using chalk pastels.
- Print a design or repeated pattern using a variety of vegetables, such as potatoes, the inside of an onion, red cabbage or a cauliflower.
- Make observational drawings of a variety of garden vegetables.
- Make clay vegetables featured in the story *Oliver's Vegetables*.
- Cut out pictures from magazines, tins and packets of different vegetables and make a collage.
- Make vegetable soup.
- Design and create a class vegetable plot in the school garden.

Mathematics

- Weigh a variety of fruit and vegetables using standard and non-standard measures.
- Create a class vegetable stall to practise weighing and money skills. Encourage the use of coin recognition, giving change and adding totals.
- Investigate halves and quarters. Give the children a selection of fruit or vegetables and pose problems, for example 'You have one apple to share between two people, four people ... .'
- Sequence and order the days of the week.
- Create a Carroll diagram by sorting vegetables according to different criteria, such as green, not green; grows underground, grows above ground.
- Collect and record data of their favourite vegetables and display as a bar chart or pictogram. Use a data handling package to present the information.

Science

- Classify vegetables according to colour, type and where they grow.
- Investigate and discuss the importance of vegetables in a healthy diet.
- Grow vegetable seeds in small pots, grow bags or the school garden. Ask the children to observe and record the changes.

Once Upon a Time

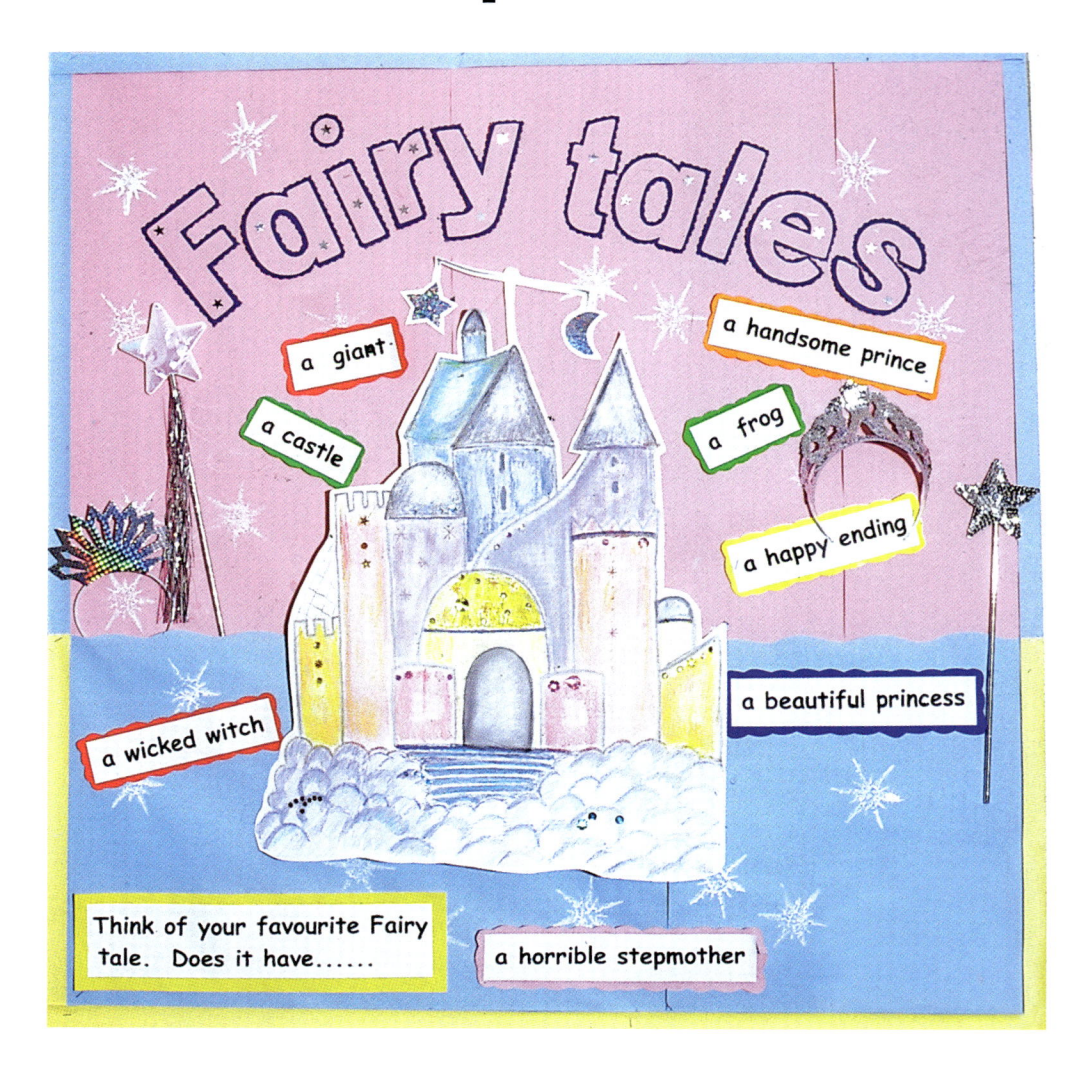

Literacy

- **Fiction:** *Once Upon a Time* by Vivian French and John Prater.
- Draw a story map detailing the little boy's day. Include all the characters from *Once Upon a Time*.
- Write a diary account of the little boy's day and the events encountered.
- Identify the nursery rhyme characters featured in the story, for example, Humpty Dumpty. Learn and recite the nursery rhymes featured.
- Play 'I-Spy' using props linked to the characters featured in the story. The children can work in pairs to identify which stories the props come from.
- Ask the children to choose a favourite character from the story. Make notes on its features and then write about that character.
- Write a letter to and receive a letter from characters from the tales in the story. Discuss with the children how to write a letter and what a letter needs, for example, a letter has an address, begins with 'Dear' and ends with 'From'.
- Rewrite one of the traditional tales featured in *Once Upon a Time* such as Goldilocks and the Three Bears, Little Red Riding Hood or Jack and the Beanstalk. Focus on a particular feature such as the way the story begins or ends.
- Ask the children to write their own fairy tale using the characteristics and features of a traditional story. It must have a happy ending, a good character and a bad character, and often animals as main characters.

Poems and Rhymes

- 'The Three Little Pigs' by Marian Swinger, *The Works* selected by Paul Cookson.
- 'Little Red Riding Hood and the Wolf' by Roald Dahl, *The Works* selected by Paul Cookson.

Art and Design Technology

- Using a variety of media, create large scale characters featured in the story *Once Upon a Time*.
- Make masks or puppets of characters from the story.
- Design and make a fairy tale castle using construction kits or recycled materials.
- Make a gingerbread house for the witch in Hansel and Gretel.
- Illustrate the nursery rhymes featured in the story.

Mathematics

- Use non-standard measures (a bean from the beanstalk or a giant footstep) to find things longer or shorter than other objects.
- Measure the height of children on a class beanstalk. Record and compare their heights and plot them on a graph.
- Build a wall for Humpty Dumpty that is higher than a table, a chair, a door or yourself!

Science

- Grow your own beanstalk by planting a bean. Record and monitor the growth of the bean over several weeks.
- Investigate ways of cooling porridge quickly for the Three Bears. Suggest ideas and test out the children's predictions.
- Investigate the strongest way to build a wall for Humpty Dumpty or the Three Little Pig's House using building bricks. Test them by attempting to knock them down.

Dance, Drama and Role Play

- According to the focus, create a role-play area to represent the Giant's castle, the house of the Three Bears or the Witch's cottage. Provide the necessary props for retelling the story.
- Create the Three Little Pigs' building site in the school grounds. Provide the children with bricks, sand, water, spades, buckets, a wheelbarrow and hard hats.

Penguins

Literacy

- **Non-fiction:** *Penguins* by Marilyn Woolley & Keith Pigdon.
- Work in small groups to record facts about penguins on large penguin-shaped paper.
- List describing words that depict life in Antarctica. Write sentences to describe the cold weather, for example, 'It's f f f freezing', 'It's c c c cold', 'It's ch ch ch chilly', 'It's sl sl sl slippery'.
- Collect penguin pictures cut from old calendars and magazines. Write speech bubbles suggesting what the penguins might be saying.
- Write a poem about penguins, saying how they move and what they do.
- Record the life cycle for another species of penguin in the same style as the non-fiction text *Penguins*. Follow the same format as for the Emperor and Fairy penguins under the headings: nesting, incubation, hatching, growing up and looking after themselves.

- **Fiction:** *Penguin Pete* by Marcus Pfister.
- Write a letter or postcard from Penguin Pete to his friend Steve explaining how he passes his time, for example, flipper skating, playing hide and seek and so on.
- Write in a diary entry format an account of Pete's day using the contents of the story.
- Create a new title for the *Penguin Pete* story. Write appropriate blurb for the backcover copy of the new title.
- Write your own *Penguin Pete* adventure relating to another of his fears or about a visit to see his friend Steve.

Poems and Rhymes

- 'Penguins' by Giles Andreae and David Wojtowycz, *Commotion in the Ocean*.
- 'Penguin' by Rebecca Clark (aged 8), *If You Should Meet a CROCODILE, Poems about WILD ANIMALS* with notes by Pie Corbett.

Art and Design Technology

- Chalk pastel penguins in different poses based on the *Penguin Pete* story.
- Paint penguins. When dry, cover with a thin coat of PVA glue to create a shiny effect.
- Print a background in cold colours onto circular-shaped paper. Make paper collage penguins and glue them on the printed background.
- Make clay penguins. Paint and varnish them.
- Make marzipan penguins and colour with food colouring. Stand each penguin on an iced biscuit.

Science

- Give each child an ice cube and challenge them to find the quickest way to melt it, for example, by holding it in their hand, putting it next to the radiator and so on.
- Investigate how to stop an ice cube from melting. Ask the children to suggest which materials they think would prevent their ice cube from melting quickly. Conduct a test to find out. Record and discuss the results.
- Take daily temperature readings and plot on a graph to find the coldest day in a week.

Information Technology

- Use the internet to research information about different species of penguin, such as the Emperor, Fairy, King, Royal and Galapagos penguins.

Geography

- Find Antarctica on a world map.
- Identify the other continents of the world.
- Locate the places where penguins live on a world map.
- Find out about icebergs. What do they look like? What are they made of?

Dance, Drama and Role Play

- In dance, create penguin movements. Huddle together to create the idea of colonies.
- Make sharp, icy movements and flat, solid, spiky shapes.
- 'Hot-seat' a penguin. The children could ask questions, such as 'What do you eat?' 'How do you sleep?' 'Do you feel the cold?'

Personal, Social and Health Education

- In the story *Penguin Pete*, Pete's mum cheers him up by giving him a treat. How do the children's parents treat them when they are feeling down?
- Penguin Pete was called 'Pint Size Pete' as he was smaller than the other penguins. Discuss the issue of name calling and consider any differences that you have that result in name calling.

Piggy Wiggy Fireman

Literacy

- **Fiction:** *Piggy Wiggy Fireman* by Chrystian Fox.
- Make a list of equipment Piggy Wiggy will need to become a fireman.
- Make a 'lift the flap' book in the shape of a fire engine. Under the flaps write the names of items that would be found on a fire engine.
- Ask the children to write a description of a firefighter or a fire engine.
- Write a story about one of Piggy Wiggy fireman's adventures.
- Design a firefighter poster, focusing on what makes a good firefighter. Refer to *Piggy Wiggy Fireman* for ideas.
- Write about a day in the life of Piggy Wiggy using a diary entry format.
- Write a newspaper report about a daring rescue or an emergency situation.
- Design a fire safety poster to tell people about the dangers of fire.

Poems and Rhymes

- 'Fire', Anon, *Poems for the Very Young* selected by Michael Rosen.
- 'Red Alert' by Gina Wilson, *Earthways, Earthwise* selected by Judith Nicholls.
- 'Power' by Moira Andrew, *Paint a Poem*.

Art and Design Technology

- Make observational drawings of fire engines using chalk pastels.
- Make a large fire engine and fire fighter collage using paper and fabric.
- Ask the children to paint a picture of their own face on circular paper or a paper plate. Add a firefighter's helmet made out of yellow paper or plastic.
- Colour-mix shades of red and yellow to paint flames for a fire picture.
- Make fire engines using junk material.

Mathematics

- Investigate capacity by finding out how many buckets or cups it would take to fill the water tray.
- Give each child a small card ladder. Ask the children to select six numbers from a bag of numbers 1–10 or 1–20 and order the numbers on the ladder.
- Place numbers written on cardboard fires around the classroom. Give each child a series of sums written on fire engines. Ask the children to find the correct fire to match each fire engine.

Science

- Set up a candle and jar experiment to show that fire needs oxygen to burn. Ask the children to predict what is going to happen and why.
- Discuss fire safety rules in school and at home.

Dance, Drama and Role Play

- Organise a visit to a local fire station or invite a firefighter into the classroom and encourage the children to ask questions.
- Act out calling for a fire engine in an emergency.
- Make a fire station. Include items for role play such as a helmet, a play axe, a bucket, a hose and a telephone. Ask the children to act out an emergency call.

The Rainbow Fish

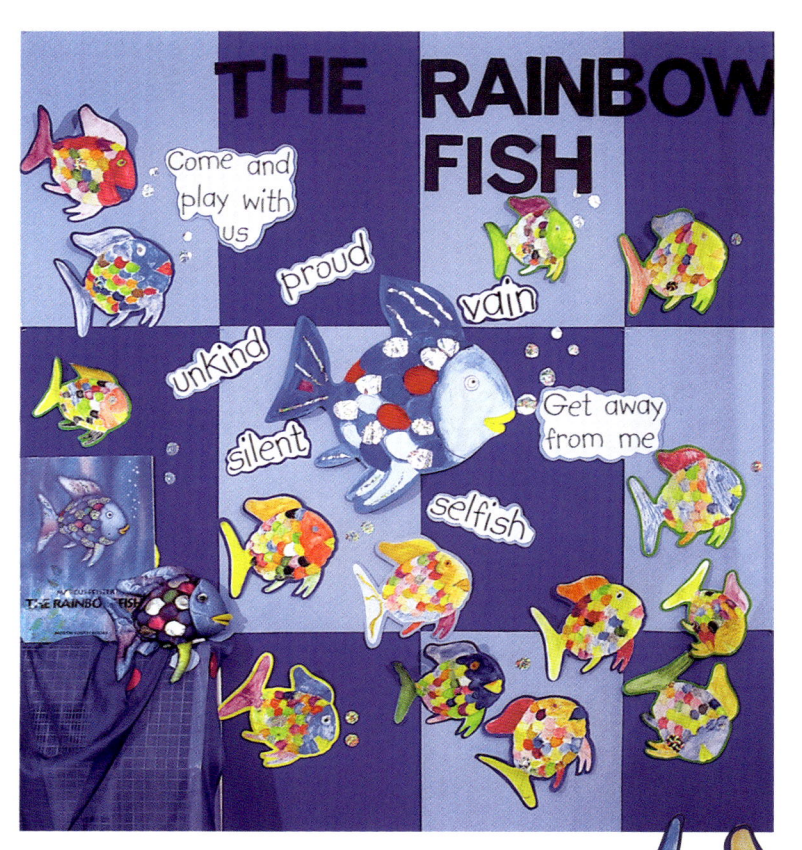

Literacy

- **Fiction:** *The Rainbow Fish* by Marcus Pfister.
- Make a story board about the Rainbow Fish.
- Use puppets to retell the story of *The Rainbow Fish*.
- Brainstorm words to describe the behaviour of the Rainbow Fish.
- Write 'sh' words on a giant laminated rainbow fish.
- Make a board game to identify 'sh' words. Laminate a large picture of the Rainbow Fish. Put a selection of 'sh' and 'ch' words on cards in a bowl or small container. Take turns to choose a card and if it begins or ends in 'sh' write it on the Rainbow Fish.
- Identify compound words such as 'rainbow'. Write the two parts of the words onto separate cards – 'rain' and 'bow', 'butter' and 'fly', and so on. Mix up the cards and match the two halves.
- Make an acrostic out of the word 'scale' to explain how the Rainbow Fish should behave towards his friends:

    Sharing
    Caring
    And
    Loving to
    Everyone

- Write a letter to the Rainbow Fish persuading him to share his scales.
- Plan and write a sequel to the story, *The Rainbow Fish*.
- Ask the children to write their own book called *The Story of the Little Blue Fish*. Retell the story of *The Rainbow Fish* from the little blue fish's point of view.

Poems and Rhymes

- 'Angel Fish' by Giles Andreae and David Wojtowycz, *Commotion in the Ocean*.

Art and Design Technology

- Cut out individual rainbow fish and use watercolours to decorate. Children can add their own silver scales.
- Use oil pastels to create a wavy, watery background. Cut out a circle and explode it to create a fish effect by cutting a 'v' shape from the circle and sticking the pieces onto the wavy background.
- Trickle PVA glue onto calico in the shape of a fish. Use fabric paint to decorate.
- Model rainbow fish out of clay.
- Design and make an underwater environment, using card, spa wood and other materials as required.
- Sketch the different types of underwater creatures that the Rainbow Fish met, for example, starfish, clams, oysters, crabs, octopus and so on.

Mathematics

- Play a fishing game. Make totals up to 10 and 20 by catching numbered card fish.
- Play a sharing game using the Rainbow Fish's scales. For example, share 10 scales between 2 children, how many scales should they each have?

Science

- Identify the different forms of sea life illustrated in the story, for example, starfish, clams, oysters and crabs.
- Draw a diagram of a fish and label the parts.
- Write fish facts on fish-shaped paper. Cover each fact with a different coloured scale. Lift a scale to reveal a fact.

Dance, Drama and Role Play

- The teacher in the role as the Rainbow Fish should wear a simple cape with lots of coloured and silver scales attached. Encourage the children to ask questions and suggest to the Rainbow Fish how he should behave. End by giving each child a silver scale.

Personal, Social and Health Education

- Discuss issues arising from the story. Why was the Rainbow Fish lonely? Why didn't the other fish like him? Have the children ever felt lonely?
- Discuss the importance of sharing and what benefits sharing can bring.

Sam's Sandwich

Literacy

- **Fiction:** *Sam's Sandwich* by David Pelham.
- Use the rhyme in the story to predict the final words on each page, saying what was in the sandwich.
- Write anagrams for the children to unscramble the gruesome ingredients in Sam's sandwich.
- Write alliterative sentences about the sandwich, for example, 'A slippery, slimy, slug on a limp lettuce leaf'.
- Write a shopping list of ingredients needed to make a particular sandwich or a gruesome sandwich.
- Write instructions about how to make a sandwich.
- Write sentences beginning, 'On my sandwich I would put ...', then list fillings in alphabetical order.
- Ask the children to write their own sandwich story, substituting Sam's name for their own. Present their work in a small book in the same style as *Sam's Sandwich*.
- Write a new story in a similar style, for example, Polly's Pasta, Ben's Bean Feast, John's Jacket Potato. John's Jacket Potato could begin, 'John filled a jacket potato with beans for his greedy sister. In the potato, he put a slimy caterpillar; on the butter, he squashed a slippery slug; in the beans, he hid a luscious ladybird.'
- Play Kim's Game. Ask the children to sit in a circle and begin their sentence with 'In my sandwich I would put...'. Each child repeats what the other children have said and then adds his or her own idea.

Poems and Rhymes

- 'Yellow Butter' by Mary Ann Hoberman, *A Packet of Poems* selected by Jill Bennett.
- 'The Sandwich' by Tony Bradman, *Twinkle, Twinkle Chocolate Bar* selected by John Foster.
- 'If You're No Good at Cooking' by Kit Wright, *A Packet Poems* selected by Jill Bennett.

Art and Design Technology

- Make a giant 'Sam's sandwich' for display.
- Ask the children to design and make their own sandwiches using collage materials.
- Make observational drawings of the salad ingredients used in Sam's sandwich.
- Paint pictures of the mini-beasts planted in Sam's sandwich.
- Make large 3D mini-beasts using recycled junk materials.
- Plan and make a healthy sandwich for lunch. What fillings could the children put in it?

Mathematics

- Investigate fractions by sharing sandwiches. Cut a round of sandwiches into halves and quarters.
- Estimate how many sandwiches can be made from a loaf of bread.
- Estimate how many sandwiches are needed for a class picnic for a given number of children.
- Add up the cost of ingredients to make a given number of sandwiches, for example, one slice of bread costs 4p, fillings cost 10p, butter costs 3p. How much would it cost to make two rounds of sandwiches?
- Conduct a survey to find out children's favourite sandwich fillings. Plot the results as a graph using a computer data handling package if desired.

Science

- Investigate the best wrapping to keep sandwiches fresh. Wrap sandwiches in different types of packaging, such as cling film, foil, a plastic bag or paper and leave for a set period of time.
- Guess the sandwich filling by using your sense of smell, taste and touch.

Dance, Drama and Role Play

- Create a sandwich bar for role play. Provide the children with items such as menus, a specials board and aprons.
- Give each child a picture of a particular food or drink, for example, ice cream, a lemon, a hot drink, soup, a banana and so on. Ask each child to imagine that they are eating or drinking their item. Other children try to guess what they are eating/drinking and whether or not they like the food by observing their facial expressions and actions.

Personal, Social and Health Education

- Discuss with the children what a healthy snack is and why we should try to eat healthy food.
- Talk about Samantha's greedy nature in the story *Sam's Sandwich*. What does greedy mean?

The Star That Fell

Literacy

- **Fiction:** *The Star That Fell* by Karen Hayles.
- Make a list of 'st' and 'ar' words. Write them on star-shaped paper.
- Write your own falling star story. Imagine finding a star. What would you do? Who would you show it to? What could you use it for? Find three uses for your star.
- Write a news report about the star that fell. Include a punchy headline.
- Write sentences about how each animal used the fallen star.
- Write a persuasive account from each animal as to why they should be allowed to keep the star.

- Do you have a box of very special things like the child in the story? What would you keep in your box?
- Rewrite *The Star That Fell* in sequence. Children can work collaboratively on large pieces of paper.

- **Non-fiction:** *I Wonder Why Stars Twinkle* by Carole Stott.
- Working in pairs or small groups, research information and write facts about stars on large star-shaped paper.
- Write sentences describing a star.
- Write a 'wish for the world' on star-shaped paper.
- Learn and recite the nursery rhyme 'Twinkle, Twinkle Little Star'.

Poems and Rhymes

- 'The Star' by Jane Taylor, *The Oxford Treasury of Children's Poems* selected by Michael Harrison and Chris Stuart-Clark.
- 'Star Wish' Anon, *The Oxford Treasury of Children's Poems* selected by Michael Harrison and Chris Stuart-Clark.
- 'The Falling Star' by Sara Teasdale, *Poems for the Very Young* selected by Michael Rosen.

Art and Design Technology

- Make salt dough stars and spray them silver.
- Sponge-print a background in shades of blue. Print silver stars onto the background. Add a sprinkle of glitter.
- Make star designs using string. Spray them silver or gold.
- Make 3D stars out of silver or gold card.
- Look at the painting *Starry Night* by Vincent Van Gogh. Recreate it using thick paint and palette knives.
- Design your own constellation.
- Make star-shaped biscuits.

Mathematics

- Make stars either by using two overlapping triangles or by extending the sides of a pentagon to form a star.

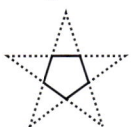

- Draw stars on squared paper. Count the squares covered by the stars to find their area.
- Investigate the properties of a star shape. How many sides does it have? How many vertices? Will it tessellate? Is it symmetrical?

Science

- What is a star? Research facts about stars.

Dance, Drama and Role Play

- Encourage the children to use their hands and whole body to create star shapes. Use gentle movements around the room, finding different levels and using different parts of the body. Work in pairs to explore mirroring, sequential movements and opposite actions. Use the music 'Oiche Chiun' ('Silent Night') by Enya, *Simply the Best Christmas*, Various Artists, (Warner ESP, 1999).
- Adopt the roles of the different animals in the story.
- Create a role play for each animal to present their reasons for keeping the fallen star. Give the star to the animal with the best argument. Encourage some disagreement and debate amongst the animals.

The Tower to the Sun

Literacy

- **Fiction:** *The Tower to the Sun* by Colin Thompson.
- Write a descriptive passage about the journey to the sun. Write about what the boy and his grandfather can see below and above, and how they feel as they get nearer to the sun.

I would get to the sun by climbing up coconut trees and a ladder. By Alex Mackenzie.

I would get to the sun by standing my statues of Liberty one on top of each other because they are so long it would be easy to climb to the top. By Ryan

- Make a list of words that rhyme with 'tower' and write them in the shape of a tower. At the top of the tower draw the sun and write words that rhyme with 'sun' in the middle.

I would get to the sun by growing a gigantic beanstalk and climb up it. By Kelly May O'Leary.

- Write a poem beginning with, 'Tower to the Sun ..., It sounds like fun! Tower to the Moon ..., Come back soon! Tower to Mars ..., They don't have cars!'
- Ask the children to describe in writing their own method of reaching the sun.
- The yellow clouds surrounding the balloon were described as 'wrapped in dirty cotton wool'. Find other ways to describe the dirty, polluted air hiding the sun.
- Write a letter asking permission to remove a famous building to be used in the tower to the sun.
- Write newspaper headlines reporting on the building of the tower to the sun, for example, 'St Paul's Cathedral, becomes first step to the sun'.
- Write a newspaper report about the building of the tower to the sun. Work in pairs, with one child as the reporter interviewing the other child. Write the article together.
- Write a diary account for Grandfather describing how he felt when he eventually saw the sun once more.

Art and Design Technology

- Use watercolour paints and pens to design your own 'tower to the sun'.
- Use fabric collage to make a giant hot-air balloon.
- Colour-mix warm colours and paint in sun shapes.
- Draw and paint some of the famous landmarks used in *The Tower to the Sun*.
- Use chalk pastels to draw sun pictures.
- Design and make a 3D tower using a wide variety of construction materials.
- Design and make a form of transport for the future. How would it be powered?

Science

- Investigate the best materials for building a tower as high as a table. Provide a variety of materials, such as cubes, tin cans, newspaper, empty boxes and sticks. Will the tower stand up on its own? Was the material easy to use? How will you join it together? Is it stable? Will it remain standing unaided?
- Discuss the importance of the sun. What would happen to life on Earth if there was no sun?

Geography

- Identify some of the famous landmarks and buildings used to build the 'tower to the sun', for example, the Great Wall of China, Ayers Rock, the Eiffel Tower, Sydney Opera House and so on. Locate these on a world map.

History

- Find out about some of the famous buildings used to build the 'tower to the sun'. Who built them? When were they built? Why were they built? What are they used for? Use the internet to support your research.

The Very Hungry Caterpillar

Literacy

- **Fiction:** *The Very Hungry Caterpillar* by Eric Carle.
- Draw a story map of *The Very Hungry Caterpillar*.
- Write sentences stating what the hungry caterpillar ate on each day of the week.
- Rewrite the story of the hungry caterpillar inside a caterpillar-shaped booklet.
- Make little words from the big word 'caterpillar'.
- Write factual statements about caterpillars. Indicate each change of sentence with a different coloured ink.
- Rewrite the story of *The Very Hungry Caterpillar* using different fruits, for example, 2 tomatoes, 4 satsumas, 6 lychees.
- Write silly sentences linked to days of the week, for example, 'On Monday I ate a banana and I changed into a monkey! On Tuesday I ate a lettuce leaf and I changed into a rabbit.'

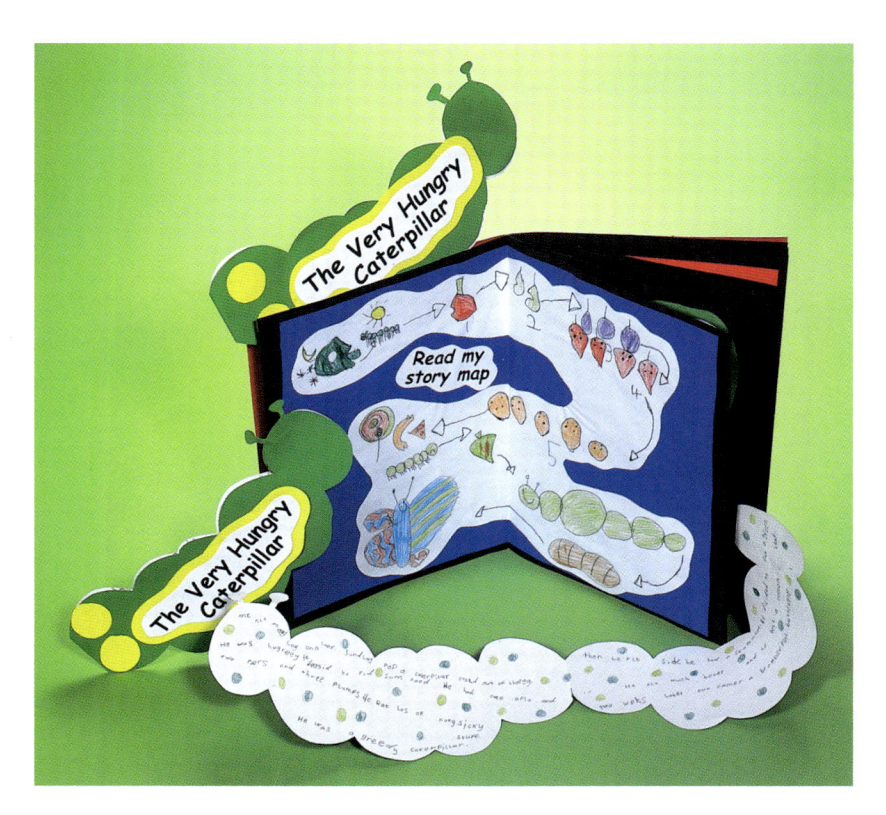

Poems and Rhymes

- 'The Tickle Rhyme' by Ian Serraillier, *Mini Beasties* selected by Michael Rosen.
- 'Message from a Caterpillar' by Lilian Moore, *Mini Beasties* selected by Michael Rosen.
- 'Caterpillars' by Mary Dawson, *The Animal Fair* selected by Jill Bennett.

Art and Design Technology

- Use fabric circles to make caterpillars and cocoons.
- Paint symmetrical shapes onto a large piece of butterfly-shaped paper.
- Paint pictures and make collage fruits and foods that the caterpillar ate through each day.
- Make a caterpillar and butterfly board game in the style of snakes and ladders.

Mathematics

- Investigate reflective symmetry by making giant butterflies and designing symmetrical wing patterns.
- Make a caterpillar number line 1–10 or 1–20.
- Cut out circles of card each with a number 1–20 and one with a caterpillar's face drawn on it. Ask the children to order the numbers correctly to make a friendly number caterpillar. Repeat for counting in 2s, 10s and so on.
- Make caterpillar measuring sticks. Use them to find the length and width of objects in the classroom.

Science

- Investigate and record the life cycle of a butterfly.
- Create a caterpillar farm in the classroom and observe the changes.

Information Technology

- Use an animation program to create a new story about the hungry caterpillar.
- Listen to the story of *The Very Hungry Caterpillar* on tape. Record your own version of the story.
- Turn a Roamer or Pixie into the hungry caterpillar and send it to items of food featured in the story.

Winter Morning

Literacy

- **Poetry:** 'Winter Morning' by Ogden Nash, *Outdoor Poems:* Big Book selected by Wendy Body.
- Read the poem.
- Discuss the meaning of 'the King of Showmen', 'tree stumps into snowmen' and 'houses into birthday cakes'. Why does the 'world look good enough to bite'?
- Identify the rhyming words in the poem. Ask the children to find other words that rhyme with 'lakes', 'white' and 'young'.

Winter Morning

Winter is the King of Showmen
Turning tree stumps into snowmen
And houses into birthday cakes
And spreading sugar over the lakes
Smooth and clean and frost white
The world looks good enough to bite.
That's the season to be young
Catching snowflakes on your tongue.

Snow is snowy when it's snowing

I'm sorry it's slushy when it's going.

Ogden Nash

- Why is Winter described as the season to be young?
- Write similes beginning with 'As cold as ...'.
- Make a list of winter weather words – freezing, icy, frosty, chilly and so on. These could be word processed using different fonts and cold colours.
- Write sentences about what you would wear on a winter's day and what you do when you are feeling cold.
- Make a list of cold things.

Poems and Rhymes

- 'Outdoor Song' by AA Milne, *Poems about Weather* selected by Amanda Earl.
- 'Sir Winter' by Jean Kenward, *Poems for Christmas* selected by Jill Bennett.

Art and Design Technology

- Colour-mix cold colours (blue, white, silver and grey).
- Make a collage using cold-coloured paper.
- Sponge-print cold colours on paper or fabric. Sprinkle with silver glitter to give an icy effect.
- Sponge-print a winter background and use charcoal to sketch winter trees from observation.
- Sew silhouettes of winter trees onto fabric.
- Paint patterns onto scarf- or glove-shaped paper.
- Illustrate a line of the poem, such as 'tree stumps into snowmen' or 'houses into birthday cakes'.
- Make ice lollipops.

Mathematics

- Match pairs of winter socks or gloves. Display with even numbers on each pair for counting in 2s.
- Sort and classify gloves, scarves and hats. Ask the children to decide on criteria for sorting, such as colour, pattern or size.
- Look at winter temperatures on a thermometer and use to investigate negative numbers. Plot the temperatures on a graph.

Science

- Investigate the best way to prevent an ice cube from melting. Wrap ice cubes in a variety of materials to find out the best insulating properties. Record your findings.
- Investigate the quickest way to melt an ice cube, for example, hold it tightly in your hand, put it in the sun or on a heater and so on. Time your experiment.
- Leave a bowl of water outside on a winter's day for 24 hours. Record the temperature of the water with a maximum/minimum thermometer.

Geography

- Identify cold climates on a world map. Colour and label them.
- Keep a weather diary for a week or a month during winter.

Book Lists

Fiction and Non-Fiction

Title	Author	Publisher	Date
A is for Africa	Ifeoma Onyefulu	Frances Lincoln	1996
The Bad-Tempered Ladybird	Eric Carle	Puffin Books	2000
Bear in a Square	Stella Blackstone	Barefoot Paperbacks	1998
Big Bad Bill	Martin Waddell	Ginn & Company	1998
Big Blue Whale	Nicola Davies	Walker Books	2001
Breakfast-Discovery World	David Flint	Heinemann	1997
A Butterfly is Born	Melvin Berger	Newbridge	1996
Charlie And The Chocolate Factory	Roald Dahl	Puffin Books	2000
The Drop Goes Plop	Sam Godwin	Hodder Wayland	1998
Elmer	David McKee	Red Fox	2000
The Enormous Crocodile	Roald Dahl	Puffin Books	1980
Fantastic Daisy Artichoke	Quentin Blake	Red Fox	2001
Frog in the Throat	Martin Waddell	Longman	1998
Greek Myths for Young Children	Marcia Williams	Candlewick Press	1992
Handa's Surprise	Eileen Browne	Walker Books	1997
Hurry, Santa!	Julie Sykes	Little Tiger Press	1999
In the Garden	Richard Powell	Treehouse Children's Books	1999
I Wonder Why Stars Twinkle	Carole Stott	Kingfisher Books	1994
The Jolly Postman or Other People's Letters	Janet &Allan Ahlberg	Viking Children's Books	1999
Jonah and the Whale	Geoffrey Patterson (Illustrator)	Frances Lincoln	1998
The Kind Christmas Tree	Anne English	Scholastic Child Education Project File	1986
Leaping Frogs: Big Book	Melvin Berger	Newbridge	1998
The Little Red Hen	Michael Foreman	Red Fox	2000
The Little Red Hen	Ronne P Randall	Ladybird Books	1993
The Little Red Hen	Margot Zemach	Red Fox	1994
The Little Red Hen and the Ear of Wheat	Mary Finch	Barefoot Paperbacks	1999
The Magic Bicycle	Brian Patten	Walker Books	1995
The Magic Porridge Pot	Joan Stimson	Ladybird Books	1993
Mrs Armitage on Wheels	Quentin Blake	Red Fox	1999
Mrs Armitage and the Big Wave	Quentin Blake	Red Fox	1999
Mrs Jolly's Brolly	Dick King-Smith	Hodder Wayland	1998
Oliver's Vegetables	Vivian French	Hodder Children's Books	1995
Once Upon a Time	Vivian French & John Prater	Walker Books	1995
Penguin Pete	Marcus Pfister	North-South Books	1998
Penguins	Marilyn Woolley & Keith Pigdon	Folens Ltd	1999
Piggy Wiggy Fireman	Chrystian Fox	Little Tiger Press	2001
The Rainbow Fish	Marcus Pfister	North-South Books	2001
Sam's Sandwich	David Pelham	Cape	1990
The Spice of Life	Kay Dunbar	Belair Publications Ltd	1992
The Star that Fell	Karen Hayles	Ladybird Books	1996
The Tower to the Sun	Colin Thompson	Red Fox	1999
The Very Hungry Caterpillar	Eric Carle	Puffin Books	1974
Zagazoo	Quentin Blake	Red Fox	2000

Poetry

Title	Compiled by	Publisher	Date
The Animal Fair	Jill Bennett	Puffin Books	1991
Another First Poetry Book	John Foster	Oxford University Press	1997
A Blue Poetry Paintbox	John Foster	Oxford University Press	2001
The Book of 1000 Poems	J Murray Macbain	Collins	1994
Centrally Heated Knickers	Michael Rosen	Puffin Books	2000
A Child's Garden of Verses	Robert Louis Stevenson	Oxford University Press	1986
Commotion in the Ocean	Giles Andreae and David Wojtowycz	Orchard Books	1999
Don't Put Mustard in the Custard	Michael Rosen	Scholastic	1996
Earthways, Earthwise	Judith Nicholls	Oxford University Press	1993
A First Poetry Book	John Foster	Oxford University Press	1979
Hard-boiled Legs – The Breakfast Book	Michael Rosen	Walker Books	2000
If You Should Meet a CROCODILE	Pie Corbett	Macmillan Children's Books	1999
Michael Rosen's Book of Nonsense	Michael Rosen	Hodder Wayland	1998
Mini Beasties	Michael Rosen	Puffin Books	1993
An Orange Poetry Paintbox	John Foster	Oxford University Press	2001
Outdoor Poems: Big Book	Wendy Body	Longman	1999
The Oxford Treasury of Children's Poems	Michael Harrison and Chris Stuart-Clark	Oxford University Press	1998
A Packet of Poems	Jill Bennett	Oxford University Press	1986
Paint a Poem	Moira Andrew	Belair Publications Ltd	1996
Poems about Weather	Amanda Earl	Hodder Children's Books	1994
Poems for Christmas	Jill Bennett	Scholastic Little Hippo	1999
Poems for the Very Young	Michael Rosen	Kingfisher Books	1996
The Puffin Book of Utterly Brilliant Poetry	Brian Patten	Puffin Books	1999
Quick, Let's Get Out of Here	Michael Rosen	Puffin Books	1985
Scholastic Collections – Poetry	Wes Magee	Scholastic	1992
A Spider Bought a Bicycle	Michael Rosen	Kingfisher Books	1999
Talking Drums	Veronique Tadjo	A&C Black	2001
Twinkle, Twinkle, Chocolate Bar	John Foster	Oxford University Press	1993
A Year Full of Poems	Michael Harrison and Chris Stuart-Clark	Oxford University Press	1996
The Works	Paul Cookson	Macmillan Children's Books	2000

Note: This list gives UK Publishers and publication dates. Readers in other territories will need to check for the local publisher.